TREND TRADING

*A Beginners Guide to Making Big
Money in The Stock Market*

Michael Jaffe

Are you confused and tired of not knowing how to enter the stock market? Which investments to buy? When to buy and when to sell? How much to invest? When and how to be out before a market crash? This book will answer these questions and more.

This simple guide will cover all the details you will need to make big money in the stock market using trend trading techniques. This process is also called swing trading. Each success factor will be explained in detail with **over 90 charts** to back up each concept. It is written in conversational style with no jargon or complicated stock talk. Each scenario will be fully explained in simple terms so you are not alone. An explanation of each buy and sell decision will be included in great detail with numerous figures so there will be no mistakes or confusion. **Each market crash since 1987 and including 2020 will be reviewed** to know when it is coming ahead of time and when to buy back at the bottom. Only the minimum amount of information you need to create incredible wealth is included. After you have mastered these principles you will only need 10 minutes a day to create your profits.

This is not a get-rich-quick scheme; there are no "secrets" but just facts that will be reviewed. These concepts are put together in a unique way to produce astounding profits. I will show you how to:

- Create winning trade after winning trade using only <u>one</u> security. That's right, only <u>one</u>.

- Succeed day-in and day-out using only <u>four</u> indicators. That's right, only <u>four</u>.

- Create double-digit returns using "Compound Investing".

- Read a stock chart in four simple steps.

- Choose what to trade, how to trade, when to trade, and how much money to trade.

- Control the emotions of excitement and fear to minimize your risk and maximize your profits.

- Choose the right time frame to generate the biggest profits.

- See, in advance, the exact day to buy and exact day to sell to generate the highest returns with no guess work using "The Rule of Many Days".

Trend Trading
A Beginners Guide to Making Big Money in The Stock Market

Copyright © 2020 by Michael Jaffe. All Rights Reserved.

Cover designed by Drew McDuffie

Visit my website at www.trendtraderz.com

Printed in the United States of America

First Printing: April 2020

This book is dedicated to two people and one group. The people are my wife, Maria, and my son, Alan. Without their patience during my "finding myself" period and during the time I was losing money day trading my success and this book would not be possible.

The group I'd like to dedicate this book to is you, my readers. I believe that anyone can achieve financial success and independence if they believe in themselves and persist. This book is written in the hope that you will be able to apply the principles inside these pages and succeed in this new endeavour.

"Believe in yourself. You are braver than you think, more talented than you know, and capable of more than you imagine."

"Instead of worrying about what you cannot control, shift your energy to what you can create."

—ROY T. BENNETT, THE LIGHT IN THE HEART

CONTENTS

Introduction. How did we get here? How trading has evolves will be reviewed with an overview of who I am and what has been my journey to success using Trend Trading. What this book will accomplish and not accomplish will be explained. Each trade with financial results will be reviewed in a chart format as a target you can aim for.

Chapter One – Factors for Success. Practical factors for success and the nuts and bolts of getting started; how to fit your job/trade/profession into the stock market process; how much time and money you will need; the frequency of trading and the best time to trade will all be explained.

Chapter Two – Trading Platforms. What trading platform to use and how to use it; how to configure your trading platform to duplicate the figures shown here with plenty of figures so you can't go wrong. You will want a platform that is device friendly – that can be used on all devices such as Apple IOS, Windows PC, and Android so you can take the device with you and not be disconnected from your trades. You will learn how to make trades and see each buy and sell signal.

Chapter Three – What to Trade. What to buy and sell; should you buy and sell stocks, ETFs, indexes, single, double, or triple leveraged ETFs, various industry groups or all of the above and the advantages and disadvantages of each,. My system will allow you to choose your venue. Here the long-term plan will be reviewed.

Chapter Four – Indicators and More Indicators. Why we use indicators, the "best" indicators to use, a few or many, how to pick and choose the ones that give consistent buy and sell signals that you can rely on and are actionable repeatedly over time.

Chapter Five – Time. An overview of time frames. Should you use hours, days, weeks, or months? What is the right one for you; what time frames work and don't work for the best results and when to buy and when to sell. We start putting it together into one cohesive whole; how the indicators work with the time frame chosen to get the biggest results. Each point will be reinforced with numerous figures and actual prices as they go up and down. You will see how easy it is to spot each buy and sell signal.

Chapter Six – Mind Over Matter. The importance of trading psychology will be discussed as well as how to set up your mind to win; how to turn off trading distractions and focus your attention only on the trade. Numerous specific examples will be reviewed from prior buys and sells so you can feel more confident in your decisions. Every major market crash since 1987 will be reviewed with pre, during, and post analysis so you do not lose money.

Chapter Seven – How to Manage Your Money. Money management will be reviewed to minimize and completely negate financial losses using stop losses, and your trading budget. How to set up a trading diary so you can keep track of your successes and failures. By reviewing the past, you can minimize mistakes in the future.

Chapter Eight – Review It All. All seven prior chapters will be reviewed to bring it all together.

Chapter Nine – Questions and Answers. Your common questions regarding trend trading related to the contents of this book are answered.

INTRODUCTION

With the advent of computers, the Internet, PCs, laptops, smartphones, tablets and associated apps, the process of stock market investing has changed dramatically. This was an industry that had insiders and outsiders. The insiders did all the work and made all the money. The outsiders, you and me, sat on the sidelines and gave our money to the insiders to "invest". Invest they did, normally in their favor. So, it is no wonder that today the industry insiders are not regarded in the highest esteem. This process can be vividly recalled during the dot-com boom and bust, the sub-prime meltdown, and many other dramatic reversals. As a result, most cash and IRA investors put their money in large investment funds with strict limits on buy and sell frequency since they didn't know any better. The goal of these large institutions was to invest your money in individual stocks (at a substantial management fee) and send you a monthly statement. Hopefully, the balance on that statement continually went up. When it did not, the investment managers recommended buying on the dip, stay fully invested, but to keep your money with them since they knew what they were doing (and we didn't) and this was complicated business best left to the professionals with their sophisticated computers and trading algorithms. I, unfortunately fell for this line.

Today, this line of thinking has not changed for most individuals with demanding or time-consuming jobs with little time to research or monitor their week-to-week investments or ordinary retirees wanting to spend time with their grandchildren or vacationing.

This has all changed for the average investor who wants to take control of his/her own investments using modern technology. But, as we all know, technology has advantages and disadvantages. When technology works, information is at our fingertips in seconds. When technology breaks down, all things stop. This can be viewed as good or bad as well, good since we can compete with Wall Street on a more equal playing field, bad since there can easily be information overload.

What then is the compromise? For me the compromise was to study, study, and study some more. I knew there had to be an easier and simpler way to make money in the stock market. I bought plenty of books and started day trading. Some years ago, I decided to take some time off from work for personal reasons and to fill that time by day trading.

A few years later and many dollars poorer I finally stopped. I had to find a better way since day trading was not working.

After some years of totally ignoring the stock market due to my losses, I started getting curious again and decided to give it another try. I knew there had to be a happy median between day trading and investing long term also known as a buy-and-hold strategy or position trading , therefore, between very short time spans and very long ones. That is when I discovered trend trading. Now let me explain. I'm not a millionaire with an abundance of free time on my hands. I am a hard-working person like you. I work long hours on my feet without much free time since I am a workaholic. I have significant financial obligations so don't have a lot of extra cash laying around. I also work a second job like many others trying to make ends meet. On top of that I have a son starting college so am very motivated to have another income stream besides my job income. So, in many ways I'm just like you. How could someone achieve a 512,400% return in nine years starting with $3,000? That is right, 512,400%! In the following pages (see Figure 1a-c below to see the numbers). I will tell you exactly how it can be achieved. It is definitely not a get rich quick scheme. It was hard work with many hours researching and experimenting. Sometimes many dollars were lost to put the concepts together that I will explain. I bought dozens of books on investing, with each one promising the "secret" to making money in the stock market and others promising that "this book is the only book you will ever need". With very book I bought there was another way to invest with none of the books overlapping in their concepts. All that was just a lot of hogwash. Part of the money I lost was buying all these books. What it did teach me was that it appeared that market investing was very complicated since each book used a different technique to investing with no two being the same which left me feeling even more confused. I had to find the right path that worked for me. Finally, I stopped cold and went back to basics.

I can tell you what I am not. I am not a professional stock market trader. I have never worked in the investment industry. I have never given investment advice professionally in any capacity to anyone except my friends. I am a regular person like each of you. Rather than finding the right strategy from others I decided to take the best ideas from each of them and develop my own system. I think that gives me a unique perspective to relay the enclosed information in a simple, easy-to-read way that will allow you to understand and implement each step of the process. A quick legal note: I am not a licensed broker or investor. This is not advice. Stock investing is a risk: you can lose your money. Please consult a licensed stock advisor before investing.

So, what exactly is trend trading, also called swing trading? No, there is no music involved and you don't dance while checking stocks. Trend trading is related to time span. Unlike day trading where a security is held for a few minutes to hours and is bought and sold that very day, trend trading is viewed in day, weeks, and months. Trend trading is also involved with watching the price of your investment trend up and down. The visual picture you will see is like watching a see-saw going up and down. You will simply buy when the price is at the bottom of the down trend and watch the price rise to the top of the uptrend, then you will sell. After you have sold (at a nice profit) you will watch the price drop again to the bottom of the down trend then you will repeat the cycle again and again. It is just that simple. There will be no need to read the business headlines every day or watch business websites or cable channels for information. That will be just a distraction. The one and only thing you will need to focus on is the price. You will buy when it is down and sell when it rises to the top and I will show you exactly how and when to do this. Take a look at the following table of results. Figure 1a-c represents what you could have earned for the three years from 2/10/2010 to 3/5/13: $3,000 to $63,594 in 14 trades. Not bad.

TQQQ	ONE DAY / TWO DAYS							AVE = 25%	AVE = 37	AVE = 53			
								4.5 trades/year					
TRADES PER YEAR	TRADES	BUY DATE	BUY PRICE	SELL PRICE	SELL DATE	PROFIT	PROFIT%	DAYS BETWEEN TRADES	DAYS HELD	START DOLLARS	NET END DOLLARS	PER TRADE $ GAIN	$ GAIN
	1	Wed, 2/10/10	1.73	2.48	Tue, 4/27/10	$0.75	43%	X	76	$3,000	$4,301	$1,301	$1,301
	2	Thu, 7/08/10	1.70	1.82	Wed, 8/11/10	$0.12	7%	21	34	$4,301	$4,604	$304	$1,604
	3	Wed, 9/01/10	1.72	2.91	Thu, 11/11/10	$1.19	69%	21	71	$4,604	$7,790	$3,185	$4,790
4	4	Thu, 12/02/10	2.94	3.83	Fri, 2/18/11	$0.89	30%	34	78	$7,790	$10,148	$2,358	$7,148
	5	Thu, 3/24/11	3.42	3.86	Tue, 5/10/11	$0.44	13%	44	47	$10,148	$11,453	$1,306	$8,453
	6	Thu, 6/23/11	3.14	3.61	Thu, 7/28/11	$0.47	15%	27	35	$11,453	$13,168	$1,714	$10,168
	7	Wed, 8/24/11	3.43	3.59	Tue, 9/27/11	$0.16	5%	10	34	$13,168	$13,782	$614	$10,782
	8	Fri, 10/07/11	2.67	3.38	Tue, 11/08/11	$0.71	27%	44	32	$13,782	$17,447	$3,665	$14,447
5	9	Thu, 12/22/11	2.80	4.93	Wed, 4/04/12	$2.13	76%	63	104	$17,447	$30,718	$13,272	$27,718
	10	Wed, 6/06/12	3.87	5.31	Mon, 9/24/12	$1.44	37%	56	110	$30,718	$42,149	$11,430	$39,149
2	11	Mon, 11/19/12	4.01	4.91	Tue, 2/19/13	$0.90	22%	10	92	$42,149	$51,608	$9,460	$48,608
	12	Fri, 3/01/13	4.72	4.98	Mon, 4/01/13	$0.26	6%	91	31	$51,608	$54,451	$2,843	$51,451
	13	Wed, 4/24/13	5.14	6.13	Wed, 5/22/13	$0.99	19%	40	28	$54,451	$64,939	$10,488	$61,939
	14	Mon, 7/01/13	5.65	6.91	Wed, 8/14/13	$1.26	22%	22	44	$54,451	$66,594	$12,143	$63,594

Figure 1-a: Potential trading results: Feb 2010 to July 2013

But wait, there is more. Due to "Compound Investing" which I will explain later, the balance in the next three years would have jumped to $1,638,895! Wow, $3,000 to $1.6 Million in 7 years, now that is impressive! How was that possible? I will explain how in the following pages.

4	15	Thu, 9/05/13	6.89	9.78	Mon, 1/06/14	$2.89	42%	31	123	$66,594	$94,527	$27,933	$91,527
	16	Thu, 2/06/14	9.48	11.28	Mon, 3/10/14	$1.80	19%	43	32	$94,527	$112,475	$17,948	$109,475
	17	Tue, 4/22/14	10.10	13.57	Fri, 7/25/14	$3.47	34%	19	94	$112,475	$151,118	$38,642	$148,118
4	18	Wed, 8/13/14	13.40	14.91	Thu, 9/11/14	$1.51	11%	40	29	$151,118	$168,147	$17,029	$165,147
4	19	Tue, 10/21/14	12.47	17.21	Fri, 12/05/14	$4.74	38%	60	45	$168,147	$232,061	$63,915	$229,061
	20	Tue, 2/03/15	15.93	18.78	Wed, 3/04/15	$2.85	18%	35	29	$232,061	$273,579	$41,518	$270,579
	21	Wed, 4/08/15	17.64	18.85	Mon, 5/04/15	$1.21	7%	9	26	$273,579	$292,345	$18,766	$289,345
	22	Wed, 5/13/15	18.18	19.36	Mon, 6/01/15	$1.18	6%	43	19	$292,345	$311,320	$18,975	$308,320
	23	Tue, 7/14/15	19.23	20.16	Thu, 7/30/15	$0.93	5%	36	16	$311,320	$326,376	$15,056	$323,376
4	24	Fri, 9/04/15	14.78	20.71	Fri, 11/06/15	$5.93	40%	102	63	$326,376	$457,323	$130,948	$454,323
	25	Tue, 2/16/16	13.22	17.70	Wed, 4/20/16	$4.48	34%	30	64	$457,323	$612,301	$154,978	$609,301
	26	Fri, 5/20/16	15.68	16.76	Fri, 6/10/16	$1.08	7%	25	21	$612,301	$654,475	$42,174	$651,475
	27	Tue, 7/05/16	15.98	20.71	Mon, 8/22/16	$4.73	30%	87	48	$654,475	$848,197	$193,721	$845,197
3	28	Thu, 11/17/16	20.75	28.80	Mon, 1/23/17	$8.05	39%	39	116	$848,197	$1,177,256	$329,059	$1,174,256
	29	Fri, 4/21/17	29.44	37.11	Thu, 6/08/17	$7.67	26%	33	48	$1,177,256	$1,483,966	$306,710	$1,480,966
	30	Tue, 7/11/17	33.62	37.13	Fri, 7/28/17	$3.51	10%	31	17	$1,483,966	$1,638,896	$154,929	$1,635,896

Figure 1-b: Potential trading results: Sept 2013 2010 to July 2017

But wait, there is more. In the next three years ending in 2019 that balance would have jumped to $15,371,813! This sounds too good to be true, but it is true! And, you will see it is true as you read further.

	31	Mon, 8/28/17	35.73	47.01	Tue, 11/28/17	$11.28	32%	16	92	$1,638,896	$2,156,297	$517,401	$2,155,297
4	32	Thu, 12/14/17	46.23	59.05	Wed, 1/31/18	$12.82	28%	14	48	$2,156,297	$2,754,257	$597,961	$2,751,257
	33	Wed, 2/14/18	51.34	59.43	Fri, 3/16/18	$8.09	16%	25	30	$2,754,257	$3,188,265	$434,007	$3,185,265
	34	Tue, 4/10/18	48.36	61.70	Thu, 6/21/18	$13.34	28%	18	72	$3,188,265	$4,067,741	$879,476	$4,064,741
	35	Mon, 7/09/18	62.78	68.68	Wed, 7/25/18	$5.90	9%	9	16	$4,067,741	$4,450,023	$382,282	$4,447,023
4	36	Fri, 8/03/18	65.33	68.60	Wed, 9/05/18	$3.27	5%	119	33	$4,450,023	$4,672,762	$222,740	$4,669,762
	37	Wed, 1/02/19	37.57	65.33	Wed, 5/01/19	$27.76	74%	56	119	$4,672,762	$8,125,408	$3,452,645	$8,122,408
	38	Thu, 6/06/19	53.14	69.42	Mon, 7/29/19	$16.28	31%	36	53	$8,125,408	$10,614,712	$2,489,304	$10,611,712
	39	Tue, 9/03/19	58.73	65.48	Thu, 9/19/19	$6.75	11%	20	16	$10,614,712	$11,834,690	$1,219,978	$11,831,690
	40	Wed, 10/09/19	59.84	77.74	Fri, 11/29/19	$17.90	30%	12	51	$11,834,690	$15,374,813	$3,540,123	$15,371,813

Figure 1-c: Potential trading results: Nov 2016 2010 to Oct 2019

You can verify these numbers for yourself by looking up TQQQ on the NASDAQ.com website on the above dates and do the math for yourself. In later chapters I will explain different styles of investing and how one is better than the others to make consistent money. In this book, I will lay out my system for trend trading for you to review. You are free to throw this book in the trash, use the tools and systems that will be reviewed, or change them to suite your individual style. One critical goal is to open your mind to a different way to look at stock market investing, a more simplified way, but repeatable day in and day out, in market upturns and downturns, during periods of bulls and busts. Only the most important information will be focused on to show you, step-by-step, how it is done. I will not include side topics that you will never need nor information that may be interesting to fill up pages but that you won't use day-in and day-out.

I ask only one thing. Do not implement or change anything in your daily life until you have read this book from cover to cover, then read it again. Take personal notes and write down your comments and impressions, both good and bad. I want you to imagine how this system could be used by you for long term gains. Start with paper trades, use a trading diary to log your wins and losses since you will have both but, definitely, many more wins. Go back 10 years in your graphing program which I will explain and slowly work your way to the present to review each concept explained here by matching the figures in this book with the graphs in your graphing program so the concepts match up. When you feel more comfortable with the process start with small money trades. Your real focus will only be the entry point and the exit point as told to you by your indicators. All you have to do religiously is do what the indicators tell you to do, period.

How to make your current job fit into trend trading, how to set up your daily routine so you have time to buy and sell without the stress of worrying hour by hour if you are making or losing money will all be reviewed. Various trading platforms will be discussed since you will need a dedicated place to buy and sell. Also covered will be what to buy and sell, what to look for when using indicators to view the strength or weakness of the price as it trends up or down. At the end of each chapter there will be a short-bulleted summary of the most important points of that chapter.

Make no mistake, this process will take time but you will need the time to digest each aspect of the process, so do not rush. This is not a get-rich-quick scheme. You can follow my plan or you can develop a plan of your own, but you do need a plan, steps a, b, and c to implement if you want to make big money in the stock market using trend trading techniques.

What WILL the information in this book accomplish?

1. Provide an extra income stream for you and your family to enjoy and, hopefully, make you financially independent.

2. Simplify the stock market process to just what you need to know to make money. There will be no jargon, complicated buy/sell plays, pennants, flags, etc. to complicate the process. This process will be as simple as 1-2-3 (but maybe 4-5 and 6 as well).

3. Each chapter will present one step in the process in simple language and easy-to-follow explanations that are built on one another. The ending chapters will bring it all together so please do not jump ahead. It will simply confuse you and, potential, lose you money.

What WON'T the information in this book accomplish?

1. Make you an overnight millionaire (but, sticking with the process over time may just accomplish that goal).

2. Provide "secrets" to trading success. Each of the chapters contains very common elements that have been around for a long time. What is unique is how these elements have been assembled to make the buy/sell process simple and easy.

3. Be the "last" book you will ever read or need on the stock market process. I do hope this does happen but doubt that it will. I doubt this for one reason. I feel every investor needs to constantly be learning and growing. You may find that this book is just the beginning of your journey or you may find that this book checks off all the boxes and stop here. The choice is yours.

So, who am I? And am I very different from you? By profession I'm a healthcare provider. Over the years I have worked in many states, venues, and over short and long time periods. I have worked in the retail, industry, and hospital sectors as an employee, manager, and supervisor. My current position provides me many perks directly suited to market trading: 1) I have plenty of time off since I work 10-hour days and work four days a week with some days off during the week. 2) I get a lunch break between 1-2pm which affords me time to check market performance each day during this break to buy or sell my positions late in the day. I only spend 10 minutes a day during this break to decide to buy, sell, or hold based on my indicators. Since I work in the Mountain time zone, I am two hours ahead of the market so 1-2pm Mountain time is 3-4pm Eastern time just before the market closes. I have adapted these benefits to my trading advantage but you can suit your personal life around the market as I have done. Just think that "I can do this" and not "I cannot do this".

The bottom line is that I'm a regular guy making significant extra money in the market while maintaining my day job which I encourage you to do as well. I guarantee your path in market trading will be filled with ups and downs after you finish reading this book. Seriously consider paper trading for the first few weeks or months to know that the principals in this book hold water and work for you regularly over time. You will need to get comfortable with each phase of the process and you can only do that with paper trades on a trading platform (software) so the prices will be updated in real time but you won't actually buy and sell. Mark each buy and sell transaction in your trading journal but don't actually make the trades so no real money will be at risk.

The reason for this is that when activating paper trading in most platforms the prices are delayed up to 20 minutes so the prices will not be accurate. In addition, you absolutely will need to back date your charts to review every trade for the past 10 years. This may sound like a lot of work but is absolutely necessary to your financial success. In your graphing program back dating means that you set a date in the past and then slowly scroll forward to the present to identify each and every buy point and sell point to condition your eyes to see the same pattern of opportunities repeated again and again. This step is crucial to your success and it does take time. If you don't take the time for this step you will not be conditioned to see these opportunities. Once your eyes are conditioned to see each buy and sell point they will jump out at you with no effort and your work will be reduced significantly and your profits will skyrocket. In this way you will minimize and even negate any losing trades. That is right, you will only have winning trades! For me, not working in the investment industry has many advantages. Here are some of them:

- I'm not biased to stocks, ETFs, markets, time frames, indicators, etc.

- All information in this book will be explained in as simple terms as possible which I would not be able to do if I was a stock market professional, therefore, no jargon or confusing concepts that you won't be using every single day.

- Since I work a day job, I am interested in extra money like you are and have written this book just to give you advice and ideas to supplement your income. If you find that you can cut your hours to part time or give up full time work altogether so much the better. I want you to succeed as I have.

My experience level is non-professional. Does this fact disqualify me from writing this book and discussing trend trading techniques? Not at all and for many reasons. First, I like what I do in my day job when working full time. My day job gives me a certain connection with others that I would not have if I did trend trade full time since trading is a solitary occupation and there are long periods when I am invested in the market and there is literally nothing to do. Second, I need another larger reason to work other than just to make money. You might call it a purpose. I need to interact with people every day so, I feel, this disqualifies me from only trading each day. I will expand more on this in the chapter on trading psychology yet I have been trading this way for many years. I have read hundreds of books on day trading, trend trading, swing trading, long term buy-and-hold strategies, etc. with mixed success. As I mentioned earlier, a few years back, I day traded and lost a significant amount of money. It was at that point that I threw away all the books and gave up. You do not want to do this since it does not make you feel good about yourself. By trial and error I learned what not to do and discovered what to do, where to do it, and how to do it. So, my past experiences and the books I read brought me to this point of success. My goal is to create a simple to understand approach which only takes a few steps and requires a minimum amount of time but which creates repeated success again and again. Hopefully, I can short circuit this process for you and bring you to my end which may be your beginning.

By buying this book I will assume each of you is also non-professional but someone who wants to learn and grow and is attracted to the stock market arena as I am. Some of the terms and concepts may be new to beginners. I encourage beginners to not be intimidated by unfamiliar terms and concepts and look up each term or idea you are unfamiliar with. My goal is to have you learn. So, keep reading and good trading!

SUMMARY POINTS:

- **Don't give up. Keep reading and ALWAYS learning.**

- **Anyone in any line of work or profession can be a success in the stock market by trend trading.**

- **Finish reading this book and practice with paper trades before starting to trade with real money.**

CHAPTER ONE

What Exactly is Trend Trading?

L et us face it. Since we live in a consumer driven economy we all want to make money, to save it, to pay off bills, to go on a long-deserved vacation, or just to spend it on stuff. It is either extra money in your part time hours or making money full time. How, then, can you make money in the most efficient way possible, by using the simplest techniques, and with the least risk to your capital? I believe the answer is investing in the stock market. Wait a minute, how is that safe and easy? I believe that it can be safe and easy. I believe that the stock market is so confusing and there is so much information on the subject that it is not easy to focus down to the most basic level and the most essential elements. I believe that the financial industry tries to keep it complicated to hang onto your money. I believe each of us needs help to simplify the process and that is where this book and trend trading comes in. As explained in the Introduction, trend trading is buying securities with the goal of holding them from a few days to many weeks or months but more than one day. Below are some stats that correspond to my paper trades over the last few years shown in Figure 1a-c:

Longest Days Held	123	Longest Days Between Trades	119
Shortest Days Held	16	Shortest Days Between Trades	9
Ave. Days Held	53	Ave. Days Between Trades	37
Ave. Trades per Year	4.5	Ave. % Gain per Trade	25%

Figure 2: Trading stats from above paper trading results Figure 1a-c

The total number of trades during this nine year period was forty. The longest and shortest trades held were for five trading days per week, Mon – Fri, so shortest was about 3 weeks and longest was about 25 weeks. These results were with the markets advancing in a sustained uptrend with some bouncing around over the last nine years. The future may be more volatile with the above averages shorter or, perhaps, longer. After you have read this book and implemented the information in it you will agree with me that these numbers are accurate. So, you see that the hold times varied significantly but were never less than 16 days or 3 trading weeks over the last nine years.

In Figure 3 below which represents an actual trending trade you will notice the buy day and the sell day corresponds to the vertical line for the date 5/20/16 (green or left line) and the vertical line for the date 1/30/18 (red or right line). This was an ETF with the symbol TQQQ with a purchase price on 5/20/16 of $15.68 and a selling price on 1/30/18 of $58.33 or +272% as viewed on a weekly chart. You can look at this same date range on the NASDAQ website to verify these results for yourself: (https://www.nasdaq.com/market-activity/funds-and-etfs/tqqq/historical). Accessed March 13, 2020.

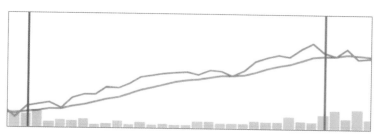

Figure 3: One buy- sell period on the weekly chart. All figures shown in this book are courtesy of Tradingview®.com

This stretch was unprecedented and achieved a profit of +272% for the 129 trading weeks invested. Again, a trading week is 5 days - Monday thru Friday. The graph length was in weeks. I usually keep my graph view set to days which I will explain a bit later. The rest of this book will focus on the principals of this one chart and many more like it.

Now, not all trades will be this profitable but you get the idea. You will note that I have averaged 4.5 trades per year. So, while I am in the trade for an average of 53 days or roughly 10 trading weeks, I am watching the price of my security increase each day for 10 weeks. I then sell as the price drops and am watching for the next move up in the cycle and the cycle continues this way up and down.

In later chapters I will review this ETF, TQQQ, (and what an ETF is) along with the indicators that go along with this chart which include the buy and sell signals. Holding securities for 53 days on average comes with some risk but I believe my system mitigates these risks to acceptable levels. By the way, everything in life is about risk and minimizing it.

A quick word about risk. There definitely is risk with investing in the stock market. There is risk everywhere you turn. Most of us handle the risk that life hands out day-to-day with no thought to it. For example, there is a health risk every day at home, play, or work. When we go on a hike we risk disaster; when we drive to work on the highway with others tailgating us there is very significant risk; there is Internet risk with our identities being stolen or by paying bills online which is very commonly done. We accept these risks every day without thinking about them because that is the price we pay for living a busy life. When we hike, we prepare ourselves to minimize the risk by wearing the proper gear, always bringing enough water with us, and never hiking alone. When we drive to work, we try to drive safely, stay to the right, and let others fly by. There is no difference with these daily risks as there is with the stock market. The key is the frequency that we are exposed to the risk. The more exposed we are the more we get accustomed to the risk until it doesn't feel like a risk at all. This applies directly to the stock market. The more you review the charts from ten years ago to the present the easier it gets to see each buy and sell point as they approach. Later in the book, I will show you how to minimize the risk of investing so the risk is, again, managed.

As explained, my average hold time has been 53 days. This fits neatly into the definition of a trend trading timeline. There is no premeditation or magic about this number. It is just the number of days that my indicators have told me to buy, hold and then sell. The alternative to trend trading is day trading which is to buy and sell in one day. At the end of that day you don't own anything. Hopefully, you have made a profit each and every day with the emphasis on hope.

Day trading has many down sides:

- It is time intensive.
- It requires deep knowledge of how to trade.
- You need to make many split-second decisions each day.
- Your personality must enjoy high stress.
- You can sleep at night even if the price of your holdings goes down suddenly.

First, you need to be available at your computer during the entire trading day, so, you can't leave and do anything else. This is not for someone who needs the income of a steady job.

Second, day trading requires a level of expertise and experience that almost all people lack except those who have committed themselves to this type of trading over a long period of time. It requires a deep knowledge of various strategies and setups that a day trader needs to know to be successful.

Third, it requires a personality that can handle high degrees of stress. I personally have learned by trial and error that I do not have this type of personality. Some days I would wake up in the middle of the night in a sweat worrying what the next day would bring. I don't encourage you to experience this feeling.

Fourth, you need to be able to handle significant gains and significant losses without being perturbed and not taking it personally. Remember, to buy, there needs to be someone on the other end making the sale and for you to sell there needs to be someone else to buy what you are selling. That is why it is called a market. In this market there are no face-to-face transaction. The buyer or seller at the other end of your transaction is anonymous. Also, and more importantly, the market does not care about you. If you lose money or make money the market does so without emotion. You are the only one adding your feelings to the transaction which I feel is a negative way to trade.

What about a buy-and-hold trading strategy? Here is the definition from Investopedia.com: "*Buy and hold is a passive investment strategy in which an investor buys stocks (or other types of securities such as ETFs) and holds them for a long period regardless of fluctuations in the market. An investor who uses a buy-and-hold strategy actively selects investments but has no concern for short-term price movements and technical indicators.*" (https://www.investopedia.com/terms/b/buyandhold.asp*), accessed March 13, 2020.*

A buy-and-hold strategy has many downsides:

- You are invested for very long periods of time, most of the time in years.
- You have very little control over your trade's profit or loss as the market goes up or down since you are in for the long term. You hope the trend over time will be up.
- Your personality must not be concerned by large moves up and down in the price of your investment over the years. With each downturn you will "buy the dip" and add more to your portfolio.
- Since the timeframe is so long you can get bored, become complacent, and not actively watch you investment as significant down trends occur.

As you can see, this is at the other end of the investing spectrum from day trading. Buy-and-hold investors have no desire to trade frequently. They are confident in their long-term strategy and don't care if the market crashes as it sometimes does. They usually view this type of event as a buying opportunity since they feel secure in the fact that the market averages will always rebound and go up again (they hope).

Trend trading has the following advantages:

- The trading time frame is long enough that you have time to wait for the buy point to come then wait for the sell point to come since there are specific days to buy and sell.
- The trading time frame is short enough that you can keep your concentration on the trade and not get bored and forget about it.
- Whether the market is in an uptrend or downtrend there are still many buying opportunities to come.
- It is easy to avoid stress since you are in the trade an average of 53 days (8 weeks) and out of the trade waiting for the next opportunity for 37 days (5 weeks) so almost 1:1.

By the way, what are you doing during the 8 weeks you are in the trade and the 5 weeks you are out of the trade? You are living your life with no stress as the market moves higher or lower. You can check in with your charts once a day for 10 minutes to see that everything is on track and then relax. With TradingView as your trading platform you can check your charts from anywhere: home, work, or while traveling. I am mentioning TradingView only as my graphing program and am not recommending this program over any other. Trend trading allows you to buy and sell leisurely and calmly. There is no problem if you wait a day to buy or sell. You may reduce your profit by a small percent but there is no other harm done. You are eliminating the emotion from the equation and can sleep at night. You may even want to skip a trade or two if there is something happening in your life such as a vacation or other event that will divert your attention. Here is an illustration of the trading spectrum between long and short with trend trading in the middle.

Trend trading will work for you since you will use specific indicators in a specific combination to verify each buy and sell transaction to maximize your entry and exit points.

Later chapters will show you each specific indicator and how to configure each one for best results. Figure 4 illustrates how trend trading works.

The lines at the bottom of each cycle indicate buy points marked "Buy" and the lines at the top of the cycles indicate sell points marked "Sell". They oscillate up and

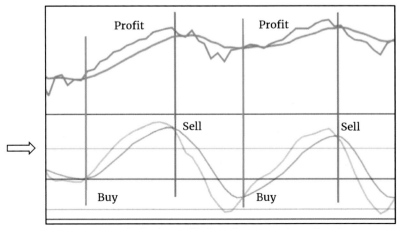

Figure 4: Typical price oscillation of two actual trend trades

down around a zero-horizontal line marked with an arrow. So, the price of this security is trending up and trending down in a regular cycle thus the name, trend trading. This illustration represents two actual trades. In these two trades there was no emotion, no hand-wringing, no sleepless nights only unemotional calm since the indicators were telling you what to do.

A later chapter will explain a number of variations to this simple trend to teach you every eventuality. Each chapter will include many figures illustrating each point so you will never be confused with any explanation.

One last thing about trend trading is that it is a form of "technical analysis" which is used to determine where the price is going (up or down) in any time frame and not "fundamental analysis". I have underlined specific words in the two quote's below.

As per Investopedia.com, "*Fundamental analysis* (FA) is a method of measuring a security's intrinsic value by examining related _economic and financial factors_. Fundamental analysts study anything that can affect the security's value, from macroeconomic factors such as the state of the economy and industry conditions to microeconomic factors like the effectiveness of the company's management. The end goal is to arrive at a number that an investor can compare with a security's current price in order to see whether the security is undervalued or overvalued." (https://www.investopedia.com/terms/f/fundamentalanalysis.asp), accessed March 13, 2020.

So, this type of study has nothing at all to do with a stock's chart and its price movement.

Alternatively, as per Investopedia.com, "*Technical analysis* is a trading discipline employed to evaluate investments and identify trading opportunities by _analyzing statistical trends gathered from trading activity, such as price movement and volume_. Unlike fundamental analysts, who attempt to evaluate a security's intrinsic value, technical analysts focus on patterns of price movements, trading signals and various other analytical charting tools to evaluate a security's strength or weakness. Technical analysis can be used on any security with historical trading data. This includes stocks, futures, commodities, fixed-income, currencies, and other securities." (https://www.investopedia.com/terms/t/technicalanalysis.asp)

For purposes of this book, we will only be discussing and using technical analysis.

SUMMARY POINTS:

- **Day trading is holding a security for one day.**

- **A buy-and-hold strategy holds a security for one or more years.**

- **Trend trading is holding a security for days, weeks, or months.**

- Focus on the price oscillation of your security to determine your buy and sell points.

- You have plenty of time to find the right buy and sell point when trend trading. Remember, there may be an exact day to buy or sell but if you miss this exact day there is no harm done if you buy or sell a day later as long as you make money.

CHAPTER TWO

Trading Platforms

What exactly is a trading platform? In essence, a trading platform is a place to buy and sell securities (stocks, ETFs, options, etc.) on your computer. There was a day when you gave your broker or banker a call to put in a trade for you. Obviously, those days are over. Now you can put in trades to buy and sell yourself with a computer. But you cannot just turn on your computer and buy a security. You need a trading platform. Think of it this way, when you go online and buy an item from eBay or Amazon, you are using their trading platform to buy and sell items. It is the same thing with securities. You are using a brokerage company to buy any number of items from the market of stocks. The brokerage companies each have unique software programs for you to log in as you do with eBay and place your order, or offer the item you own for sale. It is that simple.

There are many companies who offer trading platforms. Here is a list of a few of the top ones and to whom they are marketed to or their areas of strength:

- Fidelity Investments – Investors
- TD Ameritrade® - Traders
- Charles Schwab – Retirees
- E*TRADE® – Options investors
- Interactive Brokers – Professionals
- Merrill Edge® – Rewards programs & customer support
- TradingView - Traders

Some of you may have other thoughts about this list but it is by no means inclusive. In fact, I am sure that many of you already happily use one of these platforms. My purpose is not to sway you to another one but to show you alternatives. Each of you is the best judge of the platform you are currently using. In this chapter I will be explaining the ins and outs of the graphing software TradingView. For a variety of reasons, my actual trading account is with TD Ameritrade where I place buy and sell orders but I view charts with TradingView. TD Ameritrade also has a graphing program called thinkorswim© similar to TradingView. Of course, you will easily be able to follow along with another platform and customize it to duplicate the figures that will follow.

I use the TradingView platform for many reasons. The first is that it is easy to set up with indicators; it can be used with any browser on a Windows PC, Apple PC, Android phone or tablet, Apple iPhone, and iPad and has the same view in each device. This is very important since you want a platform that is functional and will provide you with the same data across all platforms since you are not at your PC all of the time. At various times, you will want to see the charts on your Windows PC, Android phone, or iPad and want to know that you will get the same view on each device since the view is saved online and viewed in a browser such as Chrome or Firefox. Since the database is saved online in the TradingView database, the data is identical on each device anywhere even if you don't have your own devices with you. The price for access is very modest (about $10/month while thinkorswim is free with an Ameritrade account). You can set up stop loses and buy or sell securities from each device interchangeably.

Also, I am introducing you to the graphing layout relatively early so do not be concerned. I will explain all as the chapters unfold. Once you have chosen which investment company to deal with from the above list, you will now call them at their 800 number and ask to set up an account (TradingView can be ordered and set up online). This is similar to visiting a bank to set up a checking or savings account for you except the transaction is by phone and the account is available online. Once the account is active you will link it to your checking or savings account to transfer money into your new trading account. Generally, there is no minimum amount of money needed to transfer into your new account but I would start with at least $500 or $1,000. Don't worry, everything is secure but you still have to practice prudent Internet rules of security. Once the money has been transferred into your trading account you can download the specific company's software or access the TradingView software on line in any browser. Set it up the way you want or the way I have here and start buying and selling. By the way, TradingView has relationship with some online brokerage houses so you can trade directly from the TradingView software as well.

In Figure 5-a, below, there are four areas related to price with indicators in the lower part of the screen. The top area is the price area which shows the price line as it goes up and down (1) which also includes a moving average (red line). Below that is the first indicator window (2) here showing the MACD indicator as it cycles up and down coordinating with the price movement. Below that is the second indicator window (3) showing the Stochastic Momentum indicator. Below that is the third indicator window (4) showing the CCI indicator. These indicators and more will be reviewed in Chapter Four so do not worry about them now. Below the third indicator window are the calendar days/weeks/months (5). This area can be magnified or reduced to show more days or less by scrolling up or down with your mouse anywhere in the window.

Above the chart is the bar (6) which includes the security symbol, the date, and current price, percent and dollar change for the current timeframe you are choosing to view. Moving the cursor will change these numbers for the day the curser rests on. Above this bar is the drawings bar (not shown) which has the most common drawing icons. This can be pinned or unpinned to the window for quick access.

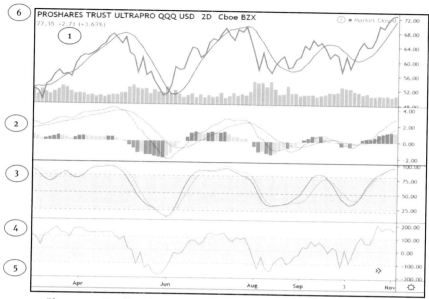

Figure 5-a: TradingView window without drawings

Figure 5-b shows the same graph as above but with no indicators. It would be almost impossible to make buy/sell decisions since you would be flying blind. This is the power of indicators added to the price.

Figure 5-b: TradingView window without indicators

In the thinkorswim software you can add a buy/sell bar. Here you can enter the number of shares to be bought or sold and place your order directly from this window without moving to another area of the program or you can log onto the Ameritrade website and place orders there. The icons here can be changed to any number of other choices. I have set up my window to have the most common icons and bars at my fingertips for ease of use.

You will notice that the price line (1) is a repeating cycle up and down identical to the price oscillation in Figure 4 above. The price goes up, the price goes down, the price goes up, the price goes down continuously and indefinitely. If you take the chart of TQQQ and go back one, five and ten years ago, the same pattern is repeated again and again - truly amazing.

This view contains all the information you will need to see if it is the proper day to buy or sell your position. You can add channels or trend lines, which I will explain later, to see if the upward move will continue or end directly from the drawing bar but, in most cases, you don't have a need for trend lines or channels since you will only rely on the price and these four indicators. These indicators also represent support and resistance points to aid in making your buy/sell decision all there at your fingertips. When added together the whole picture is one of either buy or sell. As noted earlier, one advantage of this system is that you can make your buy and then sit back and wait it out until the sell signal flashes at which time you will sell.

You can go about your daily routine with the knowledge that the move is still advancing without having to watch the chart every minute of every day.

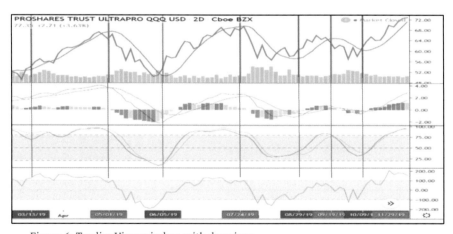

Figure 6: TradingView window with drawings

You can set up any trading platform to view similar data. I'm just comfortable with the TradingView platform from continuous use and have it set up with exactly the data I need to make my buy/sell decisions. Figure 6 shows the same view but with buy/sell lines included. This figure sure looks like Figure 4 in Chapter One. Drawings have been added to this chart to help with pattern recognition. A vertical line at the bottom of each cycle has been added to indicate a buy point and a vertical line at the top of each cycle to indicate a sell point. In addition, the buy/sell dates are also included when you add these vertical lines.

Also notice that all the indicators line up with these buy/sell lines (I have manually added these vertical lines in the indicator area to show how the upper buy/sell lines match up with the indicators). This is no coincidence. The indicators are there to corroborate the bottom and top of each cycle. This figure also matches Figure 2 so the oscillation is working as it should. The whole point of trend trading is that this oscillator repeats itself again and again to your advantage. I don't want to paint too rosy of a picture and make it seem as if there is no effort at all to making money trend trading. As we go forward in time on this chart some of the price oscillation will not be as simple as shown here since the price may be choppier and shorter in duration. That is where your training will come in with paper money. We will review each of these points in another chapter in more detail.

In the thinkorswim software you will notice the buy and sell bar (Figure 7). This is where you actually make your trades. There are three spots you need to know about. The first is the quantity space where you enter the number of shares you want to buy or sell. In this figure the number 100 represents 100 shares. The green button to the right is the buy button. Once you have entered the number of shares, you would either click the "buy" button or the "sell" button. It is that simple. You will get a chance to review the transaction before you actually make the decision to buy or sell so don't worry, you still have another chance to change your mind.

Figure 7: thinkorswim trading bar courtesy of TD Ameritrade

A word about sell stops. What is a sell stop anyway? Maybe you have seen this term in your reading. Simply, a sell stop is an insurance policy. It guarantees that if the price goes down and you are on some desert island without a computer or you are off the grid, you won't lose your shirt. Once you buy at a certain price, say $35.00, the next thing you do is place a sell stop order which is generally 2-3% below this price so $35.00 minus 2% or $34.30 and $35.00 minus 3% or $33.95. What this means is that the platform will remember your sell price and automatically execute this order without you being there if the price goes down to this price. As the price goes up, you can enter specific sell stops and delete the prior ones or enter a sell stop that automatically changes with each new price as the price goes up or down. So, in the event of a market crash you will only lose 2% or 3% and not any more. I use sell stops primarily when I know I will be unavailable to view my charts on a day-to-day basis. I will not be covering sell stops in any more detail which may vary from platform to platform. The next chapter will cover what to trade.

SUMMARY POINTS:

- You use a trading platform to buy and sell your securities. Pick one that has the features you want then set up your account and transfer in money from your checking or savings account after linking them.

- The price chart software has basic components that will not change once they are set up the way you want.

- Focus on the price oscillation of your security in conjunction with your indicators to determine your buy and sell point.

- Use sell stops as an insurance policy when you are away from your computer for an extended time.

CHAPTER THREE

What to Trade?

This is the most important question you will ask yourself. There are literally thousands of securities to choose from. You can choose individual stocks, bonds, exchange traded funds (ETFs), options, currencies, and that is just in the United States. You could trade similar securities in different countries and trade 24 hours a day, 7 days a week and go on forever! How do you narrow it down without going crazy? Well, I have narrowed it down for myself to one security. That is right, only one. I did this to keep it simple for myself since I didn't have all the time in the world to sit at my computer all day and keep track of all this data with my hard-earned money on the line. That is right, my hard-earned money. I do care about the balance in my savings account just like you do. The security I have chosen is an exchange trade index fund that follows the NASDAQ 100 market average.

First, what is the NASDAQ 100 market average? Well, this is a basket of stocks that represents technology companies. It is made up of the stocks of 100 technology companies that are traded every day. It is a market average since its price is the average of all 100 stock prices that this index represents. So, when looking at this index, you are looking at the average price of all 100 stocks. This market average includes companies like Apple, Amazon, Costco, Google, Microsoft, Netflix, Starbucks, etc. so we are talking about companies that you interact with every day. Therefore, intrinsically, this market average is much safer to trade than buying each individual stock above since it is an average of all the stocks. So, if one or two go down and others go up the market average continues to climb higher.

How exactly do you buy shares in the NASDAQ 100? Well, you don't. You have to buy a surrogate that represents all the companies in this index. That is where the ETF comes in. An ETF or "Exchange Traded Fund" is a mutual fund that trades like a stock. In this case the mutual fund we will consider contains all the stocks that are contained in the NASDAQ 100. Normally, a mutual fund from Fidelity Investments or Vanguard, for example, will allow you to buy mutual funds or a basket of stocks managed by a nal investment manager. This process of a professional investment manager managing the fund is called "actively managed" as opposed to a "passively managed" fund that you manage yourself. Traditional mutual funds can only be bought and sold a few times in a specific period. The number depends on your investment company. Both are pools of money that investors buy shares in as opposed to buying one company's stock such as Amazon or Apple.

Generally, mutual funds buy large blocks of shares in many difference companies and you buy a small number of these shares. In addition, these mutual funds contain many different stocks, some very small and volatile, not just the large company stock of the above companies. Most large mutual fund companies have what is known as a frequent trading policy. Depending on the fund, this policy may limit your ability to buy and sell these shares in the same mutual fund a certain number of times every 30 calendar days. Some companies have a limit of one trade in 60 days, that is buying and selling the same security in the same account to once every 60 days. If you wanted to trade more frequently you would be prevented from doing so. How would that fit in with the above averages?

Ave. days held = 53
Ave. days between trades: 37
Ave. trades per year: 4.5

Well, they sometimes would and sometimes wouldn't. The wouldn't part is the problem. When the market is very volatile, you may want to buy and sell more frequently than my averages above but you'd be prevented from doing so with these very large mutual fund companies.

These mutual funds have many restrictions and costs designed to have you keep your money in the fund for a long time – think buy and hold. You can buy individual stocks to trade that are in the basket of a mutual fund or you can buy an ETF. The beauty of an ETF is that it is a mutual fund (a group of stocks) that you can buy and sell on any given day without any restrictions. So, it is a mutual fund that you can buy and sell like an individual stock. And, in most cases, ETFs are commission free with most of the investment companies listed above. You are getting the best of all worlds to minimize your risk and keep the process as simple as possible. Remember, simple is best.

So, I have chosen to buy exchange traded funds or ETFs. As I just said, an ETF is a mutual fund that trades like a stock, so no frequent trading policy. This means that you can buy and sell your shares every few days if you want to so you can react to a change in price to buy and sell when your indicators tell you to and not when the investment company tells you to. Are ETFs bought and sold frequently? Well, as of May 2019, one group of investors have put $4.311 trillion into actively managed equity mutual funds like Vanguard, etc. while another group of investors, like you and me, have put $4.305 trillion into passively managed US stock market funds like ETFs, that is trillion with a T (as explained above, an example of a passive fund is one that you manage yourself vs an actively managed fund that a portfolio manager of an investment company manages for you). This is happening since a growing number of investors, again, like you and me, are realizing that money managers at these investment companies can't do better than the market averages like the DJIA, NASDAQ, etc. and in most cases do considerably worse including hedge funds that invest in anything they want including buying long and selling short. Also from Investopedia.com *"hedge funds traditionally charge 2% of assets under management and 20% of positive returns yet a study by Yale and NYU Stern economists suggested that during a six-year period, the average annual return for offshore hedge funds was 13.6%, whereas the average annual gain for the S&P 500 was 16.5%. Even worse, the rate of closure for funds rose to more than 20% per year, so choosing a long-term hedge fund is trickier than even choosing a stock investment"*. So, you can buy shares in the Dow Jones Industrial Average (DJIA) ETF that tracks the DJIA market average and achieve the same performance that this index achieves. The stock market symbol for this ETF is DJI. Take a look at the following graphs (Figure 8). The one on the right is the index (symbol DJI) while the one on the left is the ETF that tracks the DJIA called the 'DIA'. See much of a difference? I don't. All the indicators look the same and the price chart looks the same also. The only difference is that the share price of the DIA is 1/100 of the DJIA, so $268.32 vs $26,797.46. The symbol for the NASDAQ 100 index is NDX and the ETF symbol that tracks this index is QQQ and you will see the same similarities as below (Figure 9). So, if the NASDAQ 100, which you can't buy, goes up 0.5% for the day, the ETF QQQ, which you can buy, goes up 0.5% as well. Take a close look. See any difference between the following charts? Probably not.

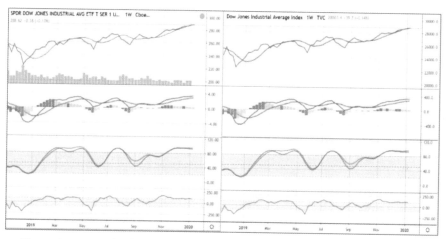

Figure 8: DIA ETF (left) vs DJIA market index (right)

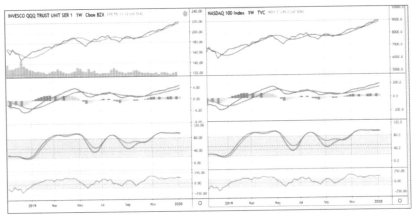

Figure 9: QQQ ETF (left) vs NASDAQ 100 market index NDX (right)

Now, I have taken this to the next level. I have chosen to buy an ETF called TQQQ that also tracks the NASDAQ 100 index just like the QQQ but instead of a 1:1 relationship between the price of this index and QQQ, the TQQQ has a 3:1 relationship to the NASDAQ 100 index. So, if the NASDAQ 100 goes up 1% for the day, the ETF TQQQ goes up 3 times this amount or 3%!

Before you get all excited, the reverse is also true. If the NASDAQ 100 goes down 1% for the day, the ETF TQQQ also goes down but 3% instead of 1% so you have to understand this before you commit to this ETF. This fact taken by itself can cause some concern, but taken in its entirety, meaning, with the above indicators and what I have shown you so far, you are minimizing the chances of a loss. In addition, by applying all the rules in this book the risk of the 1X QQQ and the 3X TQQQ are basically the same when looking at the charts. Now, if you don't understand the many principles I am teaching you and at this point go jumping into a trade the chance of a loss is very great so be patient and keep reading.

To display the above principle, look at the following two charts (Figure 10). The left one is of the TQQQ and the right one is of the QQQ. See much of difference? Actually, you won't see any difference in the charts. The price line is the same, the indicator appearances are the same, but the profit (or loss) is three times as great or 99% vs 33% for 2019! So, if you apply all my principles religiously, you should only have 3X the gains from now on. Going forward, the name of TQQQ (3:1) on each chart is called Proshares Trust Ultrapro QQQ as opposed to QQQ (1:1) called Invesco QQQ Trust so you do not get confused.

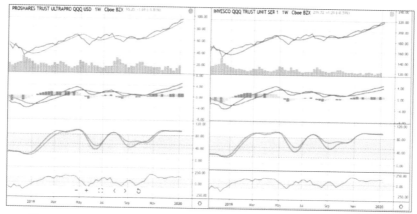

Figure 10: 3x TQQQ (left) vs 1x QQQ (right)

You may read that triple leveraged funds are unsafe, risky, not for inexperienced traders and this would all be true. But they are, in fact, safe, not at all riskier than the stock market as a whole, considerably less risky than buying individual stocks, and when you apply the principles in this book, you will not be inexperienced. While it is very true that leveraged ETFs will not create the returns you are looking for by holding them long-term, remember that your goal is not to hold them long-term but to hold them shorter-term. Remember Figure 5 from above:

Longest Days Held	123	Longest Days Between Trades	119
Shortest Days Held	16	Shortest Days Between Trades	9
Ave. Days Held	53	Ave. Days Between Trades	37
Ave. Trades per Year	4.5	Ave. % Gain per Trade	25%

Figure 5: Trading stats from above.

Your goal is this holding period of 53 days or 8 weeks on average which is the average price trend from bottom to top. Here is a definition from Investopedia.com with "trend trading" sometimes referred to "swing trading" where these terms can be used interchangeably:

"Trend trading is a trading style that attempts to capture gains through the analysis of an asset's momentum in a particular direction. When the price is moving in one overall direction, such as up or down, that is called a trend."
(https://www.investopedia.com/terms/t/trendtrading.asp), accessed March 13,2020.

And again for swing trading:

"The best way to make money with leveraged ETFs is to swing trade. That being the case, when you see a leveraged or inverse ETF steadily moving in one direction, that trend is likely to continue. It indicates increasing demand for that ETF. In most cases, the trend won't reverse until the buying becomes exhausted, which will be indicated by a flat-lining price or the price going sideways for a period of time."
(https://www.investopedia.com/terms/s/swingtrading.asp), accessed March 13, 2020.

So, unleveraged ETFs (1:1) or leveraged ones (3:1) are just as "safe" or "risky" as the general stock market. I will go one step further and say buying individual stocks can be very much riskier than buying ETFs. Here is why. Company stocks have two factors that make them much riskier:

1. First, the stock is just as stable as the business it represents. If the business is a startup or hasn't been around for a long time, or has made some unwise company decisions its future profit prospects can come into question and affect the stock price, meaning, the stock price can vacillate considerably which is not what you want. You want a price that can be reliably predicted ahead of time. ETFs like TQQQ do not have this issue.

2. Second, the price of the stock will be affected every 3 months when earnings and future business guidance is announced. Since no one publicly knows ahead of time what these results will be this can significantly affect the stock price immediately up or down without prior warning which is, again, not what you want. ETFs like TQQQ do not have this issue.

What about management fees? These are the costs the company that manages the ETF charge for you to own the ETF. According to Vanguard their average management fee is 0.3% of the funds under management. According to Fidelity their management fee is between 0.35% and 0.50%. The management fee for TQQQ is 0.95%. That sounds like quite a difference. It is but consider the profit you could make with TQQQ per $10,000 vs Fidelity or Vanguard. For the year Nov 2018 to Nov 2019 the results are in the following table (Figure 11).

FUND NAME	PROFIT %	PROFIT $	FEE %	FEE $	NET PROFIT
TQQQ	100%	$10,000	0.95%	$95	$9,905
Vanguard Total Stock Market	24%	$2,400	0.3%	$30	$2,370
Fidelity Industrials	21%	$2,100	0.35%	$35	$2,065

Figure 11: Trading stats of TQQQ vs Vanguard and Fidelity mutual funds

Even though TQQQ has a management fee three times higher than the other two, the profit minus the management fee is five times higher so the management fee compared to the profit is insignificant.

Figure 12 shows earnings, E in the circles at the bottom, for Facebook. Notice what the price does right after an earnings announcement. At #1 the price moves up then sideways for two months, at #2 the price moves down, at #3 the price moves down again, at #4 the price goes up, at #5 the price suddenly goes down significantly. There is no pattern to the price change after an earnings announcement since the earnings announcements could be good or bad so this can cause significant anxiety which you do not want.

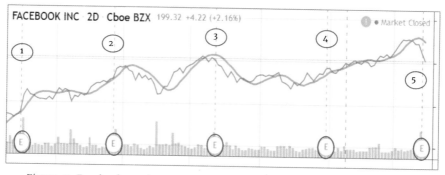

Figure 12: Facebook earnings announcements on a 2-day chart

Below is the chart for Amazon with similar results (Figure 13). Again, the price went up or down after each earning announcement with no predictable pattern. Sometimes there is an earnings surprise where the price will suddenly shoot up or down.

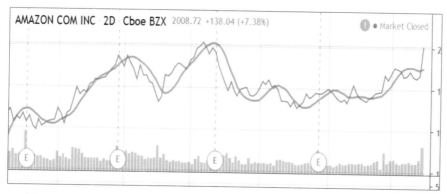

Figure 13: Amazon earnings announcements on a 2-day chart

In this case to the extreme right of the chart the price jumped suddenly higher even though the price looked like it was going to go lower just prior to the jump. We want a price that can be reliably predicted ahead of time. Look at the chart of

Figure 14: Microsoft price from July 2014 to July 2015

the following stocks for the same time periods. The first is Microsoft (Figure 14) and the second is Google (Figure 15). Both companies have been around a long time with good products that reliably produce significant profits. Both companies have strong management teams in place and a good pipeline of products that will add significant revenue to the company.

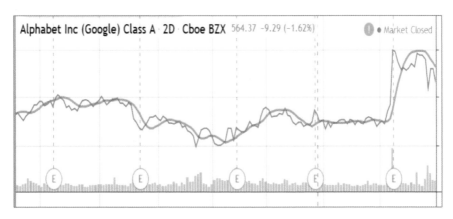

Figure 15: Google price from July 2014 to July 2015

So why does each company's stock price vacillate so greatly during the same time frame? Again, it has to do with intangibles that you and I have no control of. The price of one may be going up while the other is going down. If you owned both stocks you would have to manage each one differently and for a zero percent gain which creates complexity. We always want simple.

PRICE APPRECIATION OF STOCKS VS TQQQ

Why do we want to choose TQQQ over individual stocks? Take a look at the following stocks (Figure 16-19) and their appreciation compared to TQQQ. The percent profit for each security during the same time frame was: 25% for GOOG vs 100% for

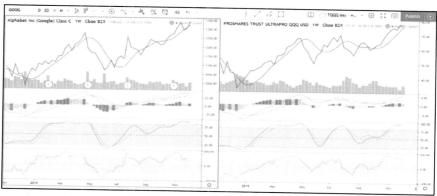

Figure 16: Google *25% vs TQQQ 100%*

TQQQ! These percentages are calculated based on the price at the extreme left of each chart compared to the price at the extreme right without regard to the price movements in between.

Look at the appreciation of the following charts compared to TQQQ (Figures 17-19). In each case TQQQ far out distanced the appreciation of the stock. Each pair may look somewhat similar but the price appreciation was significantly different.

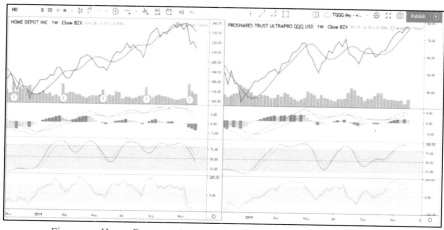

Figure 17: Home Depot *23% vs TQQQ 100%*

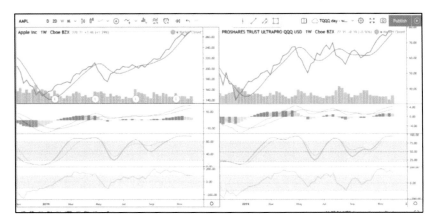

*Figure 18: Apple **39%** vs TQQQ **100%***

In these examples, don't focus on the price movement up or down. Only focus on the general appreciation from the extreme left to the extreme right. Even though all were generally moving in an upward direction so looked like they were making significant money for you, in reality, your yearly profit would have fallen far short of TQQQ.

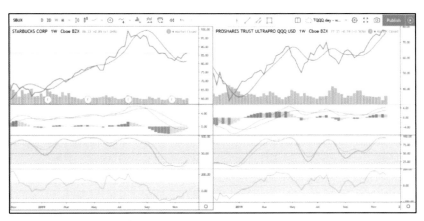

*Figure 19: Starbucks **36%** vs TQQQ **100%***

How about a comparison of very large investment company funds like Vanguard and Fidelity (Figure 20-21) with their high performance mutual funds? Again, these mutual fund shares did even worse than the above stocks.

I could go on and on. Are you starting to see a pattern here? The appreciation from all these stocks and funds are very good compared to a money market fund or a saving account but when compared to TQQQ they pale in comparison at 100% for the year

2019. You could pick any year and any portion of any year and see similar results.

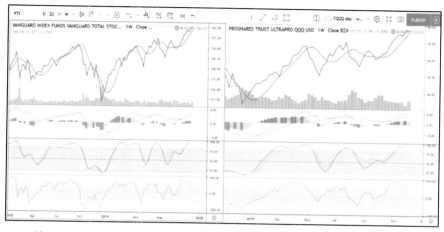

Figure 20: Vanguard Total Stock Market Fund **24%** vs TQQQ **100%**

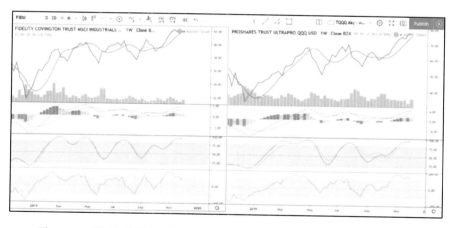

Figure 21: Fidelity MCIS Industrials Index **21%** vs TQQQ **100%**

Now you can see how it was possible to obtain the 512,400% appreciation from September 2010 to November 2019. Try it yourself, plug in the dates on your stock screener for TQQQ and see how I came up with these incredible numbers.

This appreciation is only achievable with "Compound Investing" meaning after you sell each trade, invest 100% of the proceeds into the next trade so the balance keeps climbing exponentially. It is similar to compound interest on your savings but on steroids. Now, if you wanted to take some profits off the table after you have made some real money go ahead but your total appreciation would be lower. Now I will review the parts of my plan in step order based on the above.

MY PLAN:

1. Open a brokerage account with one of the above investment companies (not a mutual fund company like Fidelity Investments or Vanguard).

2. Once opened link your checking or savings account to this brokerage account (if you need help call the investment company).

3. Transfer any amount you choose into this new brokerage account but I started with $3,000 as in Table 1a-c above.

4. Based on the information in Chapter Four below start buying and selling TQQQ with paper trades only **AFTER** you have read through this book at least once or twice and reviewed the last 10 years of trades with TQQQ.

SUMMARY POINTS:

- **Get a graphing program like thinkorswim or TradingView**

- **Rather than buying individual stocks buy ETFs**

- **Rather than buying the ETF QQQ buy TQQQ as the ETF that follows the NASDAQ 100 market average and is leveraged 3:1**

- **Start back dating by going back in time to study past buy/sell points and get comfortable with reading the graph**

- **Keep reading and studying – never stop!**

- **Don't forget practicing on paper trades to get a feel for the price movement on the graph over various timeframes**

- **Follow "The Plan"**

CHAPTER FOUR

Indicators, Indicators, Indicators

I have copied Figure 5 below as a reminder of this chart in Chapter Two. You will remember that there are three areas related to price and indicators in the lower part of the screen. The top area is the price area which shows the price line as it goes up and down (1) which also includes a moving average (red line). Below that is the first indicator window (2) here showing the MACD indicator as it cycles up and down coordinating with the price movement. Below that is the second indicator window (3) showing the Stochastic Momentum. The third window (4) shows the CCI indicator. Each of these indicators has been around for a long time and is in common use so is not a "secret" indicator that no one knows about. In TradingView you can alter the thickness of each line for each indicator to make each lighter or darker.

So, you have the following indicators:

1. Moving Average
2. MACD
3. Stochastic Momentum
4. CCI

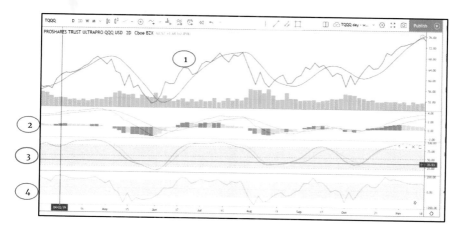

Figure 5: TradingView window without drawings

The location of these indicators on your chart can be in any order from top to bottom, except for the moving average, by just dragging and dropping each indicator up or down. The location of each has no bearing on the price or what is happening in the price section at the top. Each is a mathematical representation of the momentum of the price.

Before I begin, I want to digress for a moment and have you consider what looking at a price chart of any stock or market average represents. It represents the psychological state of mind of all the millions of individuals, mutual fund managers, hedge fund managers, etc. that are buying and selling that particular security at any given point in time all over the world. Sometimes called the balance between greed, I will call it excitement, and fear it represents the up movement (excitement) and the down movement (fear) of all those individuals. Naturally, all people want the price to go up since they are excited about making money. The market is reflected in this thinking by going up more often than going down so there is an upward bias to the market averages. But, when the market starts to go down, a herd mentality kicks in and everyone starts heading for the exits. There is mass selling since fear is in control. There is the short rebound as bottom seekers buy expecting the market to rebound but if the negative momentum continues those individuals are forced to sell at a loss or a small gain and the downward trend continues. At some point the downward trend may accelerate as IRA holders get very worried that there may be no downside limit and they also sell. See the following chart of the Dow Jones Industrial Average (DJI) stock index, the broad market average, to see what I mean starting in 2007. This chart (Figure 22) represents a -54% drop in price!

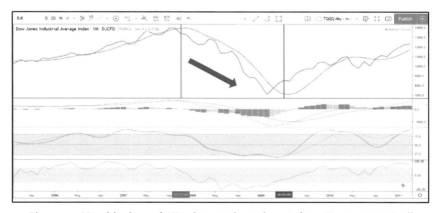

Figure 22: Monthly chart of DJIA shows a drop of -54% from Nov. 2007 to April 2009

The Dow Jones Industrial Average had been climbing from April 2003 until November 2007 and had reached a value of 14,165 at the top. Most headlines were touting the fact that the up trend could go on forever. Then, suddenly, everything collapsed until it hit a bottom at 6,547, or a -54% drop in one and ½ years. Why it stopped here is anyone's guess. But the powers that be started buying at this point. If you owned individual stocks the drop would have been just as severe for a drop of 1/2 their former value. If you had an IRA worth $100,000 with the following stocks it would have been worth $51,000 by April 2009. Quite a financial shock. Those dependent on the income from a retirement account would have been devastated. It is no wonder that the private individual was shell shocked and very reluctant to reenter the market again:

Amazon: -54%, Microsoft: -56%, Google: -58%

Here is what you would have seen in Oct 2007 using what I have taught you so far (Figure 23). At the red sell line, you would have been safely out of the market! You would have been waiting patiently for the next upturn by watching your indicators. And between Oct 2007 and April 2009 even though the market was dropping when looking at the monthly chart above and then on the one day/two day chart below there were still plenty of buying opportunities in that year and one-half to still make big money as the market was dropping. So, in up markets and down markets you can still make big money in the stock market by trend trading while others are shaking in their boots.

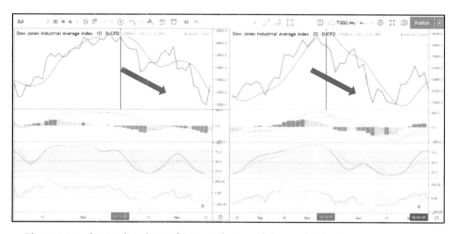

Figure 23: 1-day/2-day chart of DJIA at the top of the market in Oct. 2007

The table below (Figure 24) will give you some idea of the power of the principles outlined in this book. As the market was dropping and all the headlines were screaming doom and gloom, you were still watching your charts waiting for the next buying opportunities and there were at least four during this 14-month period. This table shows the uptrends in the NASDAQ since the numbers for the TQQQ don't go back that far. Remember that the NASDAQ percent increases will be tripled for the TQQQ which I've added to the table.

Not bad for a major down turn in the market, and the chart clearly showed these major uptrends in the overall downtrend so you would have had a +61% gain while the market had a -54% loss! Always keep this in mind when markets are trending up and down and the headlines are screaming to sell. This up and down cycle has been repeated

NASDAQ Buy Date	Buy Price	Sell Price	Sell Date	Percent	TQQQ Percent 3:1
11/27/07	2,033	2,101	12/12/07	3.3%	+9.9%
3/18/08	1,761	2,001	5/20/08	13.6%	+40.8%
7/16/08	1,844	1,909	8/19/08	3.5%	+10.5%
			TOTAL	+20.4%	+61.2%

NASDAQ Top Date	Price at Top	Price at Bottom	Bottom Date		NASDAQ Percent
10/30/07	2,239	1,037	11/20/08		−53.7%

Figure 24: Buying opportunities from Nov. 2007 to Aug. 2008 while the market was dropping

again and again and will continue as long as there is a stock market so there are always plenty of opportunities to make big money. Remember, the market is filled with abundance for those who are prepared while others who are unprepared are crying over its scarcity.

I add indicators to my current charts to verify what is happening with the price to prevent the above catastrophe from occurring. Looking at the chart (Figure 25) below, notice that each indicator rises above the top line to nearly the very top of the space that the indicator is in (horizontal black arrows on the left). This area is called the "overbought zone" since the indicator can't go higher. All it can do now is go sideways staying in this overbought zone while the price keeps moving higher. The longer the indicator is in the overbought zone going sideways, the greater the chance that the price will go down and vice versa. At some point the indicators start to turn slightly down (sell point) through the top line while the price now starts to go lower. The indicator then continues down until it meets or breaks through the bottom line (white arrow) called the "oversold zone" since the indicator can't go lower. All it can do is go sideways in this oversold zone while the price drops lower.

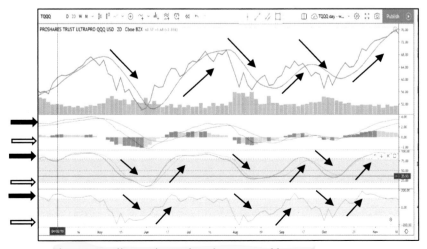

Figure 25: Indicators in overbought or oversold areas

Again, the price will either go lower, go sideways, or start to rise again as shown indicators. At some point the indicator starts to turn up (buy point) through the line and the cycle begins again.

So, "overbought" describes a period of time where there has been a significant and consistent upward move in price without much pullback. This is clearly defined by Figure 25 showing price movement from the "lower-left to upper-right" and the indicators touching or remaining in the uppermost portion of the indicator area as shown in the chart. Don't let the busyness of this chart fool you. Look at each move slowly from top to bottom and from left to right before going on to the next up or down move. You need to understand how these moves are constructed since they will be repeated again and again over the years with no stop. I have added the black up and down arrows which will not be present in your charts. When all indicators align in their movement with the price going up or down then that is confirmation that the next move is coming.

So, why these specific indicators? During my research I have tried over 300 different indicators to see which ones work best for my needs, which are the simplest in appearance, and which correlate with the price the best. I have settled on the above four. Some of the other indicators are very esoteric that individuals have invented to return certain results for them specifically. I will explain each one of the four in more detail below and why I chose it (but without too much detail or your eyes will roll back in your head).

HULL MOVING AVERAGE:

The moving average (Figure 26) is the most common indicator and provides the best correlation to the price especially since they are both overlaid on each other. The moving average (MA) is a simple technical analysis tool that smooths out the price by creating a constantly updated average price. The average is taken over a specific period of time, such as 20 days or weeks as in the chart below and those above. Since this indicator is an average of the price over the last 20 periods from one day, week, or month to the next it smooths out the sometimes jerky movement of the actual price and shows when

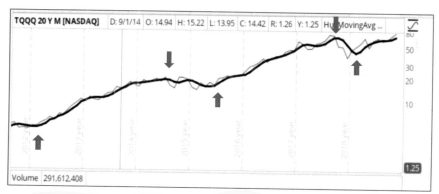

Figure 26: Hull moving average with buy and sell signals on a monthly chart

ie price is reaching a top and "rolling over" then starts to drop (down arrows) or "rolling under" to start rising again (up arrows). I have modified this indicator slightly by choosing the "Hull" option.

A short period moving average will move closely in concert with the price while a longer period moving average will react slower to the price. I like one that is shorter and reacts quicker to the price especially in a daily chart where the period is already short.

MACD

This is also called the "Moving Average Convergence Divergence" indicator (Figure 27) or MACD for short which is a trend following indicator that plots the difference between two moving averages of the price of the security that are converging or diverging as they move up and down.

The line in the graph is plotted based on subtracting a longer moving average from a shorter one. Notice that where the two lines in the indicator cross matches the light green or light red vertical lines. These crossover points indicate a buy or sell point. When the green line converges on the red line and crosses to the upside, this indicates a buy signal. As the price rises the momentum begins to slow and the green and red line begin to converge. When the green line touches the red line to begin its descent, this is a sell signal and the corresponding price will either start moving sideways or will fall.

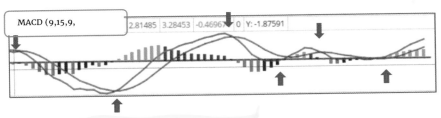

Figure 27: MACD with buy and sell signals

So far, all these indicators and the price are moving in tandem to each other which is what you want to see. This indicates that your moving in the right direction and all is in harmony (read profits!). Also notice the writing in the red circle in Figure 27: "9,15,9 weighted". These are the values to put into the indicator on your graph so it moves with the price. Doesn't this look remarkably similar to Figure 4? It is copied below so you can see the comparison.

They don't match exactly since they are from different time periods. In addition, you only see the moving average lines and not the green and red vertical bars.

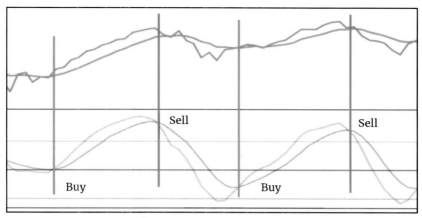

Figure 4: from pg. 16 above: Price oscillation

STOCHASTIC MOMENTUM

The stochastic momentum indicator or SMI (Figure 28) measures the distance of the closing price in relation to the midpoint or center of its high/low range. In this way, SMI is generally seen to be a more reliable indicator. SMI normally has a range between 100 and -100. Many traders will use the SMI in combination with other technical indicators, including other oscillators as I have done in all my charts. Again, the overbought region is at the top (left black arrow) and the oversold region is at the bottom (left ywhite arrow).

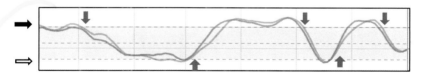

Figure 28: Stochastic Momentum with buy and sell signals

Notice how this indicator also goes up and down in correlation with the price. Above you see similar buy and sell points indicated by the up and down arrows. The settings for this indicator are 14,3,5. For a buy signal we want to see the green line go above the red line and for a sell signal the green line will go below the red line.

COMMODITY CHANNEL INDEX (CCI)

From TradingSim.com: "This indicator is an oscillator used to identify cyclical trends in a security. While the CCI will oscillate above and below the zero line, it is more of a momentum indicator, because there is no upward or downward limit on its value. The default period for the CCI indicator is 14 periods." (https://tradingsim.com/blog/commodity-channel-index/), access March 13, 2020.

ain, see the oscillation up above the lower horizontal limit line (buy) and
ow the upper horizontal limit line (sell). Again notice the values in the red
circ.   14, –100, 100" with the 14 referring to the period and the –100 and +100 referring
the upper and lower horizontal limit lines (Figure 29).

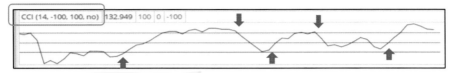

Figure 29: CCI with buy and sell signals

That is it (yeeaah)! Just these four indicators taken together in combination with
the price is all you need to complete your graph. Let me repeat the settings if you set up
your graph to look like mine (Figure 30-a & b):

The indicator settings appear when you click on the icon in the circle below
(Figure 31) and again after you have chosen the indicator and want to make changes in
the window pane by double-clicking on each indicator in the window pane.
This bar is located at the top of the graph window.

Figure 30-a: HMA and MACD settings

Figure 30-b: Stochastic Momentum and CCI settings

Figure 31: Choosing indicators and their settings

Once you choose the indicator (Figure 31), move the cursor slightly to the left and highlight the star to make it one of your favorites (Figure 32).

Choosing the indicator or double-clicking on the indicator in the window opens up the detail pane for you to change the settings.

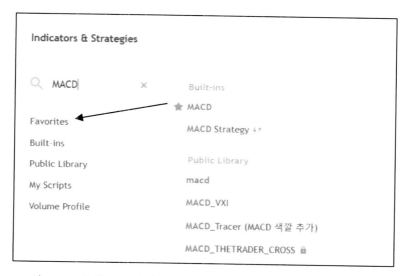

Figure 32: Indicator window opens for you to make your choice

SUMMARY POINTS:

- **Indicators coinciding with price provide buy and sell points.**

- **Indicators help visualize the price movement oscillation more clearly showing overbought and oversold areas.**

- **Consider the four indicators that work for me as your starting point.**

- **Keep it simple and don't choose too many indicators as they will just confuse you. Remember, the simpler the better.**

- **Each indicator serves to corroborate the price movement and provide the buy and sell decision.**

- Indicators work during upturns and downturns. Even during a larger downturn there are still many opportunities to make big money with upturns. Just watch the indicators for buying opportunities.

- After adding each indicator change the settings in each one to coincide with the above settings.

CHAPTER FIVE
TIME FRAMES AND OTHER PATTERNS

We always seem to come back to time in all our activities. The same is true for investing. The time frames you choose will be critical to your success or failure. Too short a time frame will have you buying and selling too frequently and most probably losing money. Too long a time frame will just translate into a buy-and-hold strategy which will have you going over the edge of Niagara Falls on more than one occasion. Either case will cause you to throw your hands up in frustration, lose money, and, in the end may even cause you to stop trading

ONE DAY CHART / TWO DAY CHART

We want a time frame that is easy to see entry and exit points. Therefore, I use two time frames in conjunction with one another: 1-day/2-day, daily/weekly, weekly/monthly. I found that the intra-day time frame (day trading) is too short for me since I don't have the time to sit around watching the chart with all the buy and sell signals which would drive me crazy. Since I work all day, I chose the one-day chart as my short time frame and the two-day chart as my longer time frame.

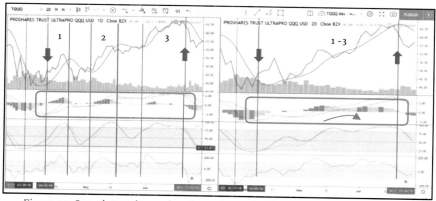

Figure 33: One-day and two-day Charts from 3/28/18 to 12/2/19

Above are my two graphs (Figure 33) as they appear in my trading software with the one-day chart on the left and the two-day chart on the right.

Notice the oblong shapes in each chart. On the left in the one-day chart the MACD indicator is moving up and down along with the other indicators with multiple buy and sell signals (green and red vertical lines I've added). Looking at the right two-day chart those conflicting signals are absent and there is only one smooth uptrend (curved arrow) with one buy and one sell signal (black arrows). The signals are magnified on the left chart. The one-day chart signals will tell you of an impending move up or down while the two-day chart will give you a wider view and tell you if those signals are valid with a desire to stay in the trade until the two-day chart start to weaken. The one-day chart signals will tell you to buy and sell three times (see the numbers) while the two-day chart will tell you to buy and stay with the purchase until the sell signal is shown for one trade. This will save you considerable stress and prevent you from being whipsawed in and out of the trade. Being whipsawed is buying and selling multiple times for an overall loss – buying too often and too late and selling too often and too late. Also notice on the two-day chart that the buy and sell signals are slightly early for the buy and slightly early for the sell for the MACD but the other indicators on this two-day chart are already showing buy and sell signals especially where the price is above the moving average. This is what you want to see so you will be making your buy/sell decisions on the one-day chart reinforced with similar indicator movement on the two-day chart.

Is it ok to buy and sell the three times as the one-day chart indicates? It is in this case. Generally, the multiple buying and selling within the one larger move could lead to trouble since some of these shorter moves may turn down more than in this chart and cause you to miss your next entry point.

INTRADAY CHARTS

Below are two charts (Figure 34 and 35) within a shorter period with intra-day timeframes meaning many multiple trades in the much shorter time period of one day.

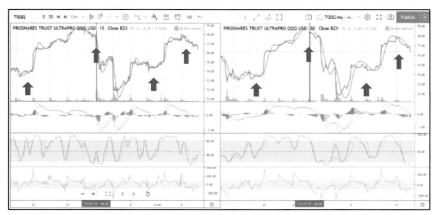

Figure 34: 15-minute and 30-minute charts from 11/22/19 to 12/9/19 or 2 trading weeks

Time frames for intra-day charts can be any time so long as the trade is opened and closed in the same day, for example, Figure 34 is for 15-minute/30-minute and Figure 35 is for 30-minute/60-minute but can be any other combination. As you can see the price line and indicators are showing buy and sell signals more suited for day trading than trend trading even though Figure 35 is 2 weeks, the chart is set to an intra-day time frame.

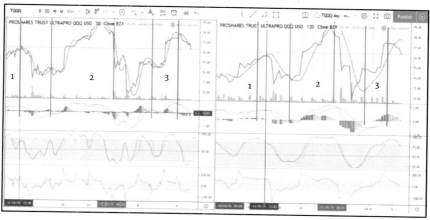

Figure 35: 30-minute and 60-minutes charts from 11/19/19 to 12/9/19

They show three buy-sell signals (1,2, and 3) in 12 trading days with a profit of 13.4%. The above charts are shown again in Figure 36 in the location of the black arrows showing the price moving sideways with the MACD pointing down. This is a period you would be out of the trade as shown by the indications. Figure 35 appears to look easy and you'd be tempted to day trade but that could lead to trouble if you attempted to trade this time frame on a regular basis since you could easily be whipsawed in and out losing money.

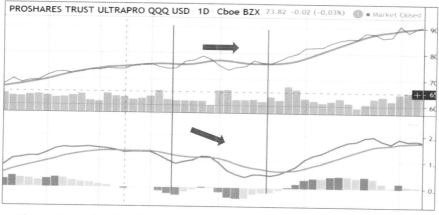

Figure 36: one day chart from 11/19/19 to 12/9/19

Looking at the same period on the 1-day chart above (Figure 36), you are in a sideways move with the MACD moving down. The dip in the middle where the black arrows are located is the same location as Figure 35 and could easily have kept going lower. On the 1-day chart we would be out of the trade until the price settled down and the indicators showed a clear buy signal which they did on 12/12/19, three days later (on the extreme right not shown). The 1-day/2-day chart gives you a longer view where the signals are much easier to see and with very much less stress so, again simpler is better.

Comparing Figure 37-a, this 30-minute/60-minute chart, with Figure 37-b, the one-day/two-day charts for the dates 10/10/19 to 12/2/19 of the same time period shows a very different picture. Now, in this chart when would you buy and sell? It looks like between five and ten times! Even I would be hard pressed to make a profit trying to choose the exact right time to buy and sell and having to stay home the entire time to not

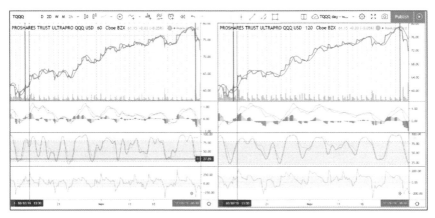

Figure 37-a: 30-minute and 60-minutes charts for the period 10/10/19 to 12/2/19

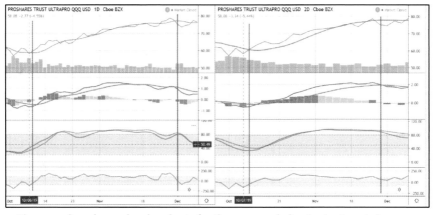

Figure 37-b: 1-day and 2-day charts for the same period 10/10/19 to 12/2/19

miss one of these signals. Now compare the 1-day chart in Figure 37-b. Need I say more?

These trades would be almost impossible unless you dedicated yourself to day trading. As complicated as this is on the intra-day chart during one smooth up period as shown in Figure 37-b it would multiply in complexity during a more difficult time when the market would be choppy with multiple ups and downs in a much shorter period. No, I will take simple over complicated any day. As I have mentioned multiple times already, simple is better (and more profitable).

WEEKLY CHART/MONTHLY CHART

The following table, Figure 38-a, sums up the results from May 2018 to Oct 2018 but in the weekly format with the buy/sell lines included in Figure 38-b. Tell me if you see what I see, namely, that the buy and sell signals appear too late.

Weekly Chart Buy Date (Fig.34)	Buy Price	Sell Price	% Gain
5/7/18 – 10/01/18	$55.50	$64.75	**16.7%**

Figure 38-a: One-week chart

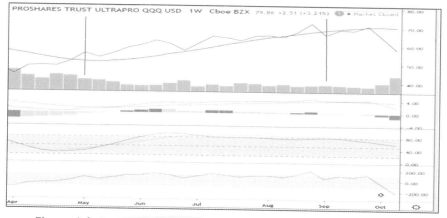

Figure 38-b: One-week chart from 4/11/18 to 9/5/18

Now look at the daily table (Figure 39-a and corresponding chart (Figure 39-b). Instead of buying on 4/11/18 at $45.36 (one-day chart) you would have bought on 5/7/18 at $55.50 (one-week chart) or 29 days later and 18% higher. The sell signal would have occurred on 9/5/18 at $68.60 (one-day chart) vs on 10/1/18 at $64.75 (one-week chart) and 5% lower, in addition you would have had three buy/sell signals for three profit opportunities on the one-day chart rather than just one profit opportunities on the weekly chart. That would translate into a profit of 48% on the daily chart vs 17% on the weekly chart. Quite a difference.

Daily Chart Buy Date (Fig. 35)	Buy Price	Sell Price	% Gain
4/11/18 – 6/20/18	$45.36	$63.34	39.6%
7/9/18 – 7/23/18	$62.78	$65.10	3.7%
8/3/18 - 9/5/18	$65.33	$68.60	5.0%
			48.3%

Figure 39-a: Daily charts

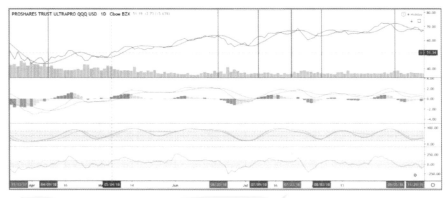

Figure 39-b: One-day chart from 4/11/18 to 9/5/18

So, the same problems confront us with periods that are too short or too long in that the returns are lower for both, the buy/sell signals are either too frequent or not frequent enough, and with either too many trades or not enough trades. In my opinion the stress levels are the same in the longer time frame since the market is going lower faster than the chart is indicating so you are watching your price drop before receiving the sell signal. With the shorter time frame, the multiple buys and sells would make you frazzled and have you up at night with the high probability that you would lose money with the whipsaws up and down. Both are not pleasant and much more complicated.

Sometimes the weekly chart is what you want to watch and not the daily if your stress level is low. See the following table (Figure 40-a & b) that lists the results on the weekly chart (a) which shows five moves up between 7/5/16 to 10/1/18 for a total of +127.2% and compare that to the daily chart (b) that list thirteen trades for a total of +234.5% for a +108% difference.

In table "b" the shorter the time frame the higher the profit. This works since the above date range is one of a generally sustained uptrend but even in short ups and downs the shorter time span will generate higher profits due to the delay built into the longer time span charts (a). This delay can cause problems since it gets you into the trade late and, more importantly, gets you out of the trade late. Buy the way, the thirteen trades in 26 months translates into 6 trades a year, not too different from my average of 4.5 trades per year. Again, if your stress level is low go with the weekly chart and be happy with the 127% profit in 26 months which is very respectable.

Weekly:	Price Gain	% Gain	Total % Gain
7/5/16 – 10/17/16	17.28 – 21.08	22%	
12/5/16 – 3/20/17	21.58 – 28.26	48%	
4/24/17 – 6/5/17	31.78 – 34.42	17%	127.2%
10/2/17 – 1/29/18	39.78 – 54.06	51%	
4/30/18 – 10/01/18	51.19 – 64.75	39%	

Figure 40-a: Weekly vs daily profit

Daily:	Price Gain	% Gain	Total % Gain
7/5/16 – 8/16/16	15.98 – 20.61	29.0%	
9/19/16 – 10/10/16	20.46 – 21.69	6.0%	
11/16/16 – 3/3/17	20.28 – 28.43	40.2%	
4/21/17 – 6/9/17	29.44 – 37.11	26.1%	
7/10/17 – 7/28/17	33.34 – 37.25	11.7%	
8/29/17 – 9/20/17	36.17 – 38.123	5.4%	
9/29/17 – 10/20/17	38.08 – 40.59	6.6%	234.5%
10/27/17 – 11/30/17	42.86 – 45.70	6.6%	
12/12/17 – 1/30/18	46.06 – 58.33	26.6%	
2/13/18 – 3/16/18	48.50 – 59.04	21.7%	
4/9/18 – 6/20/18	45.36 – 62.04	36.8%	
7/5/18 – 7/24/18	58.45 – 65.93	12.8%	
8/3/189 – 9/5/18	65.33 – 68.60	5.0%	

Figure 40-b: Weekly vs daily profit

Another problem with longer period charts is that you never know when the end of the move will begin and, if it starts, you never know how deep the drop will be. See Figures 41-43 for periods of significant price drops that were generally not predicted. With my buy/sell system using the one-day/two-day charts you are locking in your gains with each trade by assuming that the end of that trade will always be the beginning of the next major trend down. If the trend continues up, great, you are on your way toward higher profits.

If it ends you are safely on the sidelines while others are watching their profits disappear. So, in most cases the market will be much choppier and with an associated increase in frustration and potential for a significant drop if using the weekly or monthly chart. That is why I stick with a shorter time frame of the daily charts. Look at the following examples of an unexpected drop. In each case you would have been safely out of the market waiting for the next buy signal. When they occur, price drops occur suddenly and without warning from different dates and with significant percent drops in price so you have to observe and respect the sell signals when they occur. My rules will always keep you out of trouble.

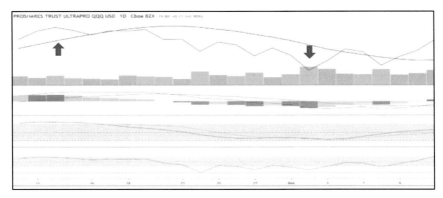

Figure 41: TQQQ Daily chart: High on 9/12/19 of $65.98 to a low on 10/2/19 of $59.04, a drop of -11% in 15 trading days or 3 calendar weeks

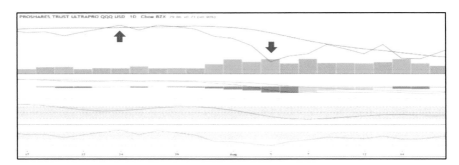

Figure 42: TQQQ Daily chart: High on 7/24/19 of $70.05 to a low on 8/5/19 of $55.24, a drop of -21% in 9 trading days or 2 calendar weeks

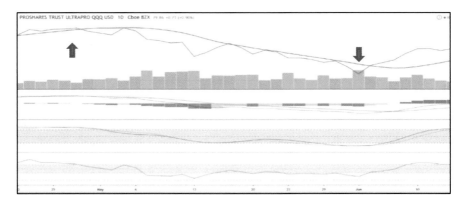

Figure 43: TQQQ Daily chart: High on 5/3/19 of $67.57 to a low on 6/3/19 of $47.01, a drop of -30% in 22 trading days or 4 calendar weeks

In your learning phase don't be upset if you occasionally miss the sell signal and get out a few days late during the start of these painful down trends. It's part of the cost of doing business in the stock market. Over time, these missed sell opportunities will no longer occur and your profits will skyrocket.

CONSOLIDATION

There is a larger cycle that I'd like to present as another tool in your arsenal. Rather than seeing the market price just go up and down with no rhyme or reason, there is a larger picture that presents itself. Notice the following table of the weekly chart. Use the weekly chart to zoom out for the bigger picture and see the bigger trends, then zoom back in to the 1-day/2-day charts to see where you are in that bigger trend to make multiple trades but always be respectful that you are in a period of consolidation (Figure 44). What it shows is a large move up, then a period of sideways movement called consolidation, then another move up, then more consolidation, again and again. The consolidation may include large moves up and down which eventually level off to start the next move up. You can make plenty of money during these consolidation periods as the price moves up and down in a sideways fashion but the up and down moves are sharper with short bursts up and down so it is much more demanding and you will have to pay very close attention.

Move:	Time interval:	Price Move:	Percent up or down:
Up	8/2010 – 2/2011	1.65 – 3.83	132%
Consolidation	2/2011 – 1/2012	3.83 – 3.58	-8%
Up	1/2012 – 4/2012	3.58 – 5.02	+40%
Consolidation	4/2012 – 4/2013	5.02 – 5.08	+1%
Up	4/2013 – 7/2015	5.08 – 21.00	+313%
Consolidation	7/2015 – 11/2016	21.00 – 21.00	0%
Up	11/2016 – 1/2018	21.00 – 60.66	189%
Consolidation	1/2018 – 5/2018	60.66 – 60.14	-1%
Up	8/2018 – 9/2018	60.14 – 72.30	+20%
Consolidation	9/2018 – 10/2019	72.30 – 72.30	0%
Up	10/2019 - present	72.30 – 79.25	+10%

Figure 44: Up moves with periods of consolidation

Then the uptrend that follows is much smoother and easier to stay within the next longer trend up with the consolidation starting again. You will see this type of pattern repeated again and again so anticipate it rather than rebel against it. Remember, the market doesn't know you nor does it much care about you. It is very impartial so go with it. Use it to your advantage.

The consolidation periods (sideways move) may contain big moves up and down which are relatively hard to buy into and sell out of using the weekly chart since the time frame of this chart is too long so, again, use the daily charts during the uptrends and consolidation periods to make repeated trades for very high profits.

During consolidation periods there are significant moves up and down for solid trades and plenty of money to be made when viewed in the daily chart. There follows a period of sideways movement with no gain or loss. Then the up-trend starts again with the move very easy and regular.

Notice the repeating pattern in the weekly chart in Figure 45 with ? On the monthly chart, being slower, will show just three consolidation periods with three up periods rather the six shown here. This is telling since if you only trade from the monthly chart you will miss much of the money that can be made since the monthly chart is basically a buy-and-hold strategy. The shaky price line (red circle below) during the uptrend on the weekly chart translates into significant, numerous, and more profitable moves up on the one-day/2-day chart but looks like one smooth uptrend on this chart.

In addition, in this chart see another significant buy and sell signal, namely, three double tops (1,2, and 3) and two double bottoms (A and B). The bottom to the right of #1 is not a double bottom but a "V" shaped bottom. What are these and of what significance are they? Double tops psychologically mean that buyers are concerned that the price may have moved too high too soon and are having second thoughts about the upward trend continuing.

At the first top they start getting cold feet and the price drops (Figure 46). They then push their confidence to create the second or even third top but there are more sellers than there are buyers and the price drops again but this time significantly as shown by the large down moves. The same thing happens at a bottom. For some reason that eludes us, the selling suddenly stops and buyers enter the market. The sellers try again to keep the prices moving down but the buyers also try again and the next time succeed in driving the price up and a large upward trend begins again. Just as there are buyers hoping that the price will continue higher, there are also sellers called short

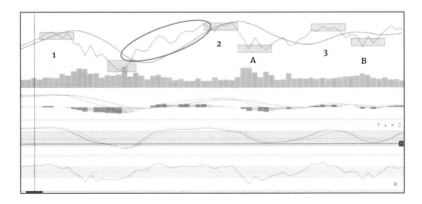

Figure 45: Weekly chart: Consolidation periods present buy and sell opportunities

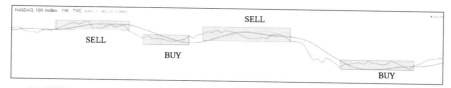

Figure 46: Weekly chart: Consolidation periods present buy and sell opportunities

sellers hoping to make money when the price drops. These short sellers can drive the price down sharply and swiftly so a sustained gain can be erased in 25% of the time that it took to create the uptrend. These drops occur suddenly and violently so you have to always be on the lookout for them to occur. At a bottom these short sellers are in battle with the buyers to see who will win since each wants to make money with the price moving down or the price moving up. During this period the price will move sideways in a tug of war called a consolidation pattern as is shown in the above table and charts. On a shorter chart these consolidation periods occur all the time since the price can't go up in a straight line. Be prepared for the price to go up, then across, then down, then across, then up again. Also, notice that when the consolidation starts after a large move up, the next move is down and vice versa.

This pattern will be repeated continuously. On a longer monthly chart these consolidation periods will be less visible but will be there visually when the price reaches a peak before a major drop.

In Figure 46 and 47, each sideways consolidation as the price moves up and down is a net 0% gain or loss in each green box on the weekly chart. This marks the battle that is ongoing between the buyers and sellers to determine the next move up or down. Here it is, below, during the financial crisis in 2007 where the price dropped -51% for the NASDAQ which would have been a -153% drop on the TQQQ!

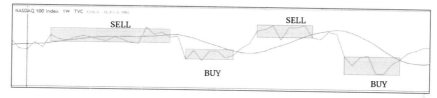

Figure 47: Weekly chart: Consolidation periods present buy and sell opportunities

STEP PATTERNS

Another pattern you will see again and again will be the Step Pattern. This pattern can be present either as the price is dropping or climbing with each presenting numerous buying opportunities along the way. You can see this pattern on a weekly chart (below). In Figure 48, the price drops in four steps for a total of –83% (–246% on the TQQQ) from #1 to #4.

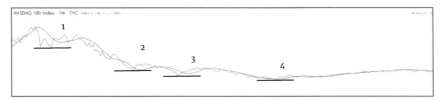

Figure 48: Weekly chart: Step pattern with price dropping

Here it is again on the weekly chart (Figure 49) but moving up with a percent rise of +127% from #1 to step #4 and onto the extreme right of the chart (+381% on the TQQQ).

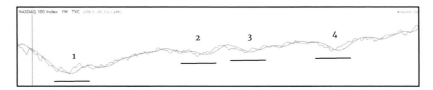

Figure 49: Weekly chart: Step pattern with price rising

Here it is again on the daily chart (Figure 50) and a 5-step rise with an increase of +89% (+267% on the TQQQ) from #1 to #5 and beyond. Each of these arcs up is another buy and sell trade. These huge percent increases are how that 512,400% profit could be achieved.

Figure 50: Weekly chart: Step pattern with price rising

DOUBLE AND TRIPLE TOPS AND BOTTOMS

As I have explained above, double and triple tops and bottoms are very common and very useful for you to determine the direction of the market. Looking at Figure 51, each arrow shows a double top or bottom. A double or triple top will signal that the price is going lower (arrows pointing down) with a triple top more powerful than a double top. This indicates resistance to the price going higher. If these occur while the price is dropping it signals that there is support to prevent the price from dropping further and the price generally rises and is called a double or triple bottom (arrows pointing up).

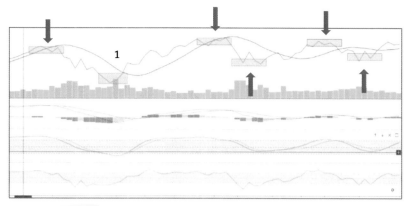

Figure 51: *Weekly chart of Figure 42: Consolidation periods present buy and sell opportunities*

Again, a triple bottom is more powerful than a double bottom. As you can see, at double tops the price has gone lower and at double bottoms, the price in each case has gone higher. The bottom at #1 is a "V" shaped bottom and not a double. Remember, we are dealing with human psychology so if traders believe that a double or triple bottom means that the price will not go lower, then it does not and the reverse is true for a double or triple top so it is a self-fulfilling prophecy.

SUPPORT AND RESISTANCE

Support and resistance points act as barriers to prevent the price from going lower or rising higher. In Figure 52, resistance represented by the top vertical lines prevent the price from going higher. We added these lines to the two highest point on the graph. As the price hits this high point once, twice, or three times the price will either bounce off of this imaginary line and go lower or suddenly move higher. In most examples, the price moved lower in the case of the top resistance and higher in case of the bottom support.

Support, represented by the lower vertical line, occurs when the price has dropped and suddenly stops. It then goes up again and then goes down again and stops at the same price. This is a strong indicator that this is the bottom of the move down and may signal an entry point for the price to rise.

I'm presenting many alternatives to buy-and-hold, namely, week/month, day/week, and one-day/two-day alternatives. Play with each combination and see which one works best for you and your temperament. There are no wrong answers only the right answer for you that makes you money and allows you to sleep at night. Remember, until you settle on one set of time frames you must use paper trades and back date the graph to see what the price did at an earlier time.

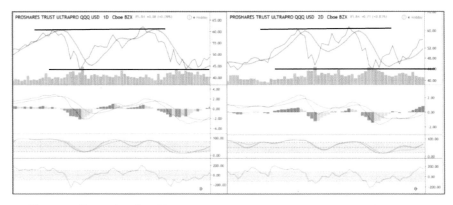

Figure 52: Support and resistance

You can do this easily with TradingView. This time frame process took the longest for me to settle on so expect it to take a while for you also. For me, the real money to be made is using the one-day chart with a side glance at the two-day chart to see that I am still on track as I have explained above.

Occasionally, there will be very large moves down as happened in 2000-2003 during the dot.com bust (-81%), 2007-2008 (-47%) during the financial crisis which coincided with economic recessions and a smaller but still significant one in 2018 (-17%) but these down moves are few and far between but which I will review later in great detail. Remember that these percentages are for the market index NASDAQ but the percent drop would be three times greater for TQQQ so -242%, -141% and -51% so you'd want to avoid these drops at all cost. Average investors with a buy-and-hold strategy would sit through these staggering losses and say, "the market will regain these losses since it always moves up". They may even "buy the dip" at each pause and invest more money as the price continues to decline. Remember that the purpose of investing is to make money regularly not make money then lose it all then make it back for a net zero return. For the period following the 2000-2003 drop it took 15 years to go from 4,705 to 833 and back to 4,705! For the 2007-2008 drop it took 4 years to go from 2,239 to 1,180 and back to 2,239! That is a total of 19 wasted years with no income! We are also assuming that this average investor would immediately reinvest at the bottom and would know when the bottom was reached which is not very realistic. In reality, this investor would have been so rattled by the drop that he would perhaps wait at least another year or more to put his money back in, if at all. So more wasted years and much longer to recoup his losses. Some investors would realistically have sworn off the stock market altogether never to return.

I don't want that for you. With some simple planning and much study by implementing the steps outlined here you can prevent these catastrophic losses and rest easy at night while everyone else is going crazy.

TRENDLINES AND CHANNELS

Trendlines and channels are formed when the price is headed consistently in one direction up or down. It is best seen on the 2-day chart and repeats again and again so is a very handy tool to use regularly. There is a drawing tool in TradingView to draw these. When the price is headed up or down, the trend wants to continue in the same direction over time.

This time period can be short or long but either way, a reversal is inevitable. Figure 53 illustrates this concept. As you can see, once the trend starts heading down it continues until a point is reached when the trend starts to reverse (vertical lines). Where the price breaks above the downward headed trendline is your buy point. It also should coincide with your indicators giving a buy signal. The same is true as the price heads up. Where the price breaks below the upward trend line is your sell point and, again, it coincides with the story your indicators are telling you at this point, namely, sell. You may notice that as the price heads up, it stays in a very narrow range, not vacillating much up or down. This is a characteristic of large price movements such that a channel can be drawn to anticipate this continuing movement. The price going down or up continues in a very narrow range until the trend is broken. Your indicators coincide with this price change so it is not too hard to tell whether you should buy or sell.

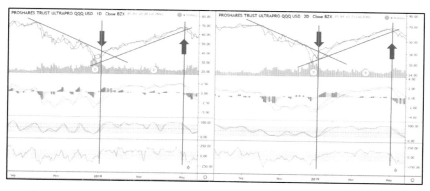

Figure 53: Trendlines on the 1-day/2-day chart show when a trend is starting, continuing, and ending

The channels are drawn on the same charts (Figure 54) in place of trend lines with a channel drawing tool. It is important that you respect the break of the price below the upper trend line since in this chart the price dropped -44% at the far right but you would have been safely out of this trade.

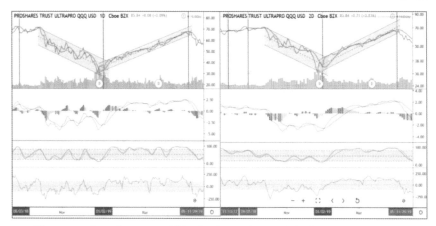

Figure 54: The price stays within the channels until it is time to buy or sell

MID-MOVE INDICATOR

One unusual secondary indicator that I have found being repeated again and again is a mid-cycle correction that usually shows itself at the half way point in an up or down move. It has repeated itself 28 times from 2010 to 20019 or three times a year so almost with every move up. See the chart below for one example. Again, this is repeated on average 3 times per year so is a very reliable indicator. The move up in Figure 55 started on 6/3/19 and continued until 7/25/19 or about 7 weeks. At approximately the mid-point of the move, 6/25/19 or week 3, this dip started (arrow).

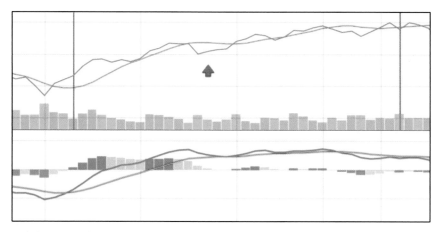

Figure 55: The arrow shows the mid-move indicator about half way up the move

Here it is again (Figure 56) on 3/1/18 within the move that started on 2/8/18 until 3/15/18 or at week 3 in a 6 week move.

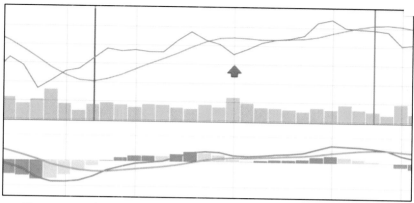

Figure 56: On the 1-day chart the arrow shows the mid-move indicator about half way up the move

In the 28 times this mid-move indicator has presented itself the averages show that once the upward move started 5 weeks later this mid-move correction showed up followed by another 5 weeks until the up move ended. This is a downward feint meant to scare investors out of the up move so sophisticated traders can buy more shares at the expense of the smaller players at a Lower price then move in and continue the move up until it ends. These other players do not represent you or me but larger institutional players. With the frequency and regularity of this move, it certainly is worth watching and waiting for it and not falling for this distraction by selling.

Notice the same move on the 2-day chart (Figure 57) as the above 1-day chart for the same date range. Here the price did not even break below the moving average and does not register on the MACD indicator which keeps you in the trade. This is why I always look at the 2-day chart for corroboration before buying or selling.

HOW TO PROFIT IN A DOWN MARKET

Now to change topics slightly I will ask you what you would do with your money during the above major negative drops in the market? One solution is to sit tight and stay in a money market account, or just plain cash.

Wouldn't it be great if you could make money as you would when the market was going up but also make the same amount of money while the market was going down? Well, there is a solution to make an equal amount of money when the market is tanking. There is an ETF that mirrors the reverse of the TQQQ called SQQQ with an almost mirror image of the loss transformed into a gain which is also triple leveraged as is TQQQ. This ETF goes up when the market is going down and down when the market is going up so its value occurs only when the market has reached a significant or climax top, which I will discuss shortly, and is about to crash. For example, in 2018 when the

TQQQ dropped -54% in 3 months the SQQQ went up +50% during the same period. Not bad!

Look at the following table (Figure 58) for a comparison of these two ETFs during the last three really bad times in the market:

Major Downturns	TQQQ	SQQQ
2000 – 2003	-242%	+239%
2007 – 2008	-151%	+149%
2018	-51%	+50%
	-444%	+438%

Figure 58: TQQQ vs SQQQ during three major downturns

SQQQ showed an equal and opposite move to the positive for each of TQQQs moves to the negative. But be careful when using SQQQ and only hold this in reserve if 1) the market has reached a climax top which occurs during an extended uptrend when the price suddenly shoots way up at an unsustainable angle then in a few days suddenly shoots down and 2) when the price has had a sustained uptrend then starts moving sideways in a consolidation phase then starts dropping (Figure 59-a).

This is a classic signal that the market has run out of steam and will fall significantly. This is the only time when you want to consider selling TQQQ and buying SQQQ otherwise stick with TQQQ. Below is a more current example of this type of drop that had occurred on 2/19/20. The uptrend started on 10/10/19 with the price at $61.15 and reached a climax top on 2/19/20 with the price at $118.06 or +93% in four months, WOW! I've blocked out the next change in direction with the blue vertical boxes to not give away the next move after this date.

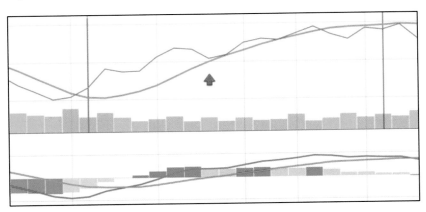

Figure 57: The same move on the 2-day chart

By the way, at the very edge of the blue boxes you'll see that your indicators were starting to flash a sell signal at the arrows (see the MACD and the price dropping below the moving average on the one-day chart).

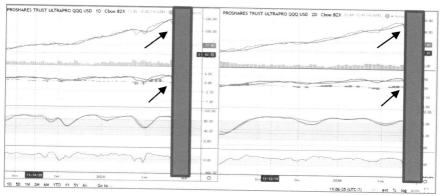

Figure 59-a: TQQQ at a climax top

Here is what happened next with the blue boxes removed (Figure 59-b). The TQQQ price dropped from $118.06 to $77.00 or -34% in 7 days or almost one-half of the gain in only one week, YIKES! Now see what SQQQ looked like during the same period (Figure 60). In this figure, on 2/19/20 the price was $15.99 and on 2/27/20 it was $23.76 or +49%!! In this case it was well worth it to switch from TQQQ to SQQQ but you would have to watch it carefully since SQQQ could drop just as fast as TQQQ could go up.

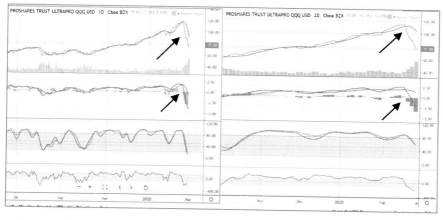

Figure 59-b: TQQQ at a climax top rolling over

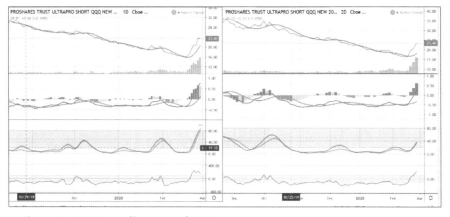

Figure 60: SQQQ at a climax top of TQQQ

SUMMARY POINTS:

- Timeframes can be long or short. Very short intraday timeframes are for day traders and very long ones are for buy-and-hold investors. A one-week chart timeframe will get you in and out of a trade too late resulting in reduced profits. Use the 1-day and 2-day chart timeframes to view price movement that is most accurate for four to five trades per year where you will capture virtually all upward moves.

- Consolidation periods occur when the price has just concluded an up or down move and is now moving sideways before the next leg up or down which is best seen on the weekly chart. Step patterns occur when the price moves up or down in a step-wise pattern indicating a pause in the movement before the next move up or down. Be on the lookout for double and triple tops and bottoms as they preview the next move down or up.

- Support and resistance lines are your visual cue that the price may not go lower during support and may not go higher during resistance.

- Trendlines and channels visually show continuing movement up or down until the price breaks above or below the channel lines signaling a change in direction.

- Consider buying SQQQ when the TQQQ has moved up in a climax top and may drop precipitously very soon.

CHAPTER SIX

Mind Over Matter

Does psychology enter into our buy/sell decisions? Should this be part of the conversation in making or losing money in the stock market? Does fear and excitement enter into the buy/sell equation? The answer to these questions is a resounding yes. Human psychology is a significant factor in making and losing money in all areas of life especially the stock market. As we discussed earlier, the excitement and fear of potentially making and losing money in the stock market is graphically expressed in the price graph of any stock and the market as a whole. If there were no emotions, it would feel like a so-so job you were going to daily for the last twenty years – boring. The excitement of making money can be exhilarating and a loss can feel devastating. This is why many people shy away from investing in the stock market. These emotions are multiplied when knowledge is lacking. We feel like we are out on a limb and don't know how to get down or, worse yet, may fall and break our necks. I'm writing this book first and foremost for you to gain knowledge. In the beginning I mentioned that I'd like you to read this book from cover to cover, perhaps put it down for a while then read it again before doing anything. Let the ideas I have covered percolate and steep over time so your curiosity is stimulated. Only then will you be in a place to learn. In addition, slowly review each section in each chapter again and again while looking at your charts and duplicating each figure.

Repeating this exercise is a must to remembering the current visual cue that you have seen this chart pattern before. Go back and find a similar pattern in the past as you are seeing now. Find more repeating chart patterns again and again to force your memory to remember a past chart pattern repeated in the present.

Individuals who allow their emotions to make financial decisions will result in very poor long-term results. One emotional feeling is the "fear of missing out". Suppose you are watching the one-day/two-day graph of TQQQ and it suddenly starts to rise. All the indicators are flashing that the price will start rising shortly. You look over at the two-day chart and see a similar result but you hesitate. You say to yourself, "I'm not sure. I had better wait a bit longer until the uptrend is showing more clearly." As the price starts to rise some days later you feel that maybe your decision to wait was the wrong one but then you think that, perhaps, it may be too late and the price is moving away from you. Look at the following chart (Figure 61) on buy day and the next one (Figure 62) if you waited.

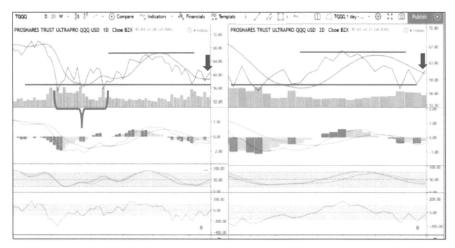

Figure 61: 1-day/2-day chart: Look at the far right of each chart. Should you buy?

In Figure 61, see the arrow on the left 1-day chart; the price is above the moving average; it appears that each of the indicators are turning up; a quick look at the right 2-day chart looks like it is a little early since the two-day chart does run a little early but the price is touching the moving average (arrow). The price here is $59.84. You also see a triple bottom (bracket) at this price that was mirrored in a triple bottom some months earlier. The price at the quadruple bottom in the 1-day chart (horizontal line) is saying this is the bottom and the price will rise.

Now see Figure 62 where the right-hand vertical line and arrows in each chart represents where the arrow was in Figure 61. The point to enter was correct but now the price seems to be running away from you. What to do, what to do?? The price here is $65.92 or 10% higher! This is the point that your "fear of missing out" emotion gets in control and you buy late. Then in Figure 63 on the left chart, the price starts to stall (arrow) and, OMG, you made a mistake or so your emotional mind tell you. The left hand chart 1-day of Figure 63 shows the price potentially about to drop at $64.16 (arrow). Is it too late? Will the price drop or will it keep going higher? Then you make mistake #2, you sell even though the right-hand 2-day chart still looks good and all the indicators are on solid ground. Then in Figure 64 the price continues up and you buy it back but at $68.49. Your emotionally all over the place. What you aren't doing is making money unemotionally.

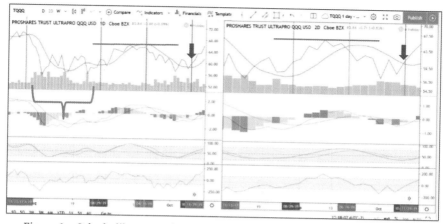

Figure 62: It looks like you waited too long. Should you buy late?

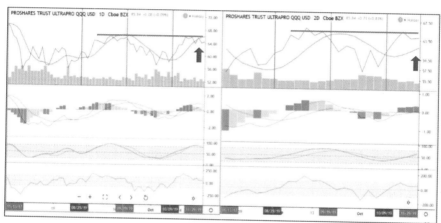

Figure 63: How about now?

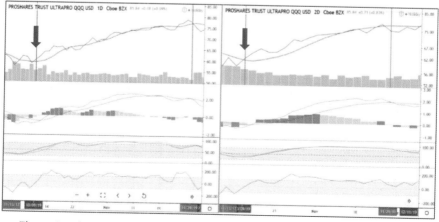

Figure 64: The price kept going much higher!

Figure 64 confirmed that the price kept going all the way to $77.74 with the arrows showing the point you were at in Figure 61 when you should have bought at $59.84 and held.

Would you have made money or lost money? Would you have gotten in at the correct price or later at a higher price? As you can see, in real life situations, your "fear of missing out" can work for and against you. In Figure 61 the correct decision was to buy. All factors were pointing to this being the correct point of entry. In Figure 63, the price on the 1-day chart had increased but was coming to a point of resistance potentially forming another double top where the price could stall. In fact, Figure 63 looked just like the price would stall on the 1-day chart but on the 2-day chart all the indicators were pointing to higher prices ahead. By losing confidence and waiting, then selling, then buying back again your profit would have totaled +11%. If you had originally bought at $59.84 and held until $77.74 your profit would have totaled +30%, quite a difference. Without the confidence that comes with trading for a while and familiarity with past patterns just like this one, your emotions would be in control leading you to potentially costly decisions. Imagine this scenario repeated 4-5 times a year. Your profits would be considerably lower and your confidence would be correspondingly lower as well.

The opposite of the emotion of "fear of missing out" is the "fear of losing everything". This is the emotion that hits buy-and-hold "investors" that see a major correction coming but do nothing about it. The price starts dropping but never stops. Finally, near the bottom this "investor" decides to sell just when it is time to buy since the price is at the bottom. In the context of this book, this fear is less important since you are well on your way to having the confidence to get out of your trade before it is too late and, by now, you are definitely not a buy-and-hold investor.

The psychology of the market can be seen every day while watching the evening news. If the market is rising you will see a big green arrow pointing up and the change in large numbers corresponding to the daily point rise of the Dow, S&P, and NASDAQ market averages. On the Internet business websites you will see traders rejoicing as the markets go higher and fearful as the markets head lower (Figure 65).

Figure 65: Traders rejoice or in fear as the markets head higher or lower. Images courtesy of CNBC

These are all signals that sway you emotionally one way or the other that the markets will never stop going up or will crash spelling the end of humanity. Even a tweet from a President can cause markets to go up or down with no data to support the move. We have to stay clear of all these emotional pitfalls. I don't watch the daily news but get my daily information from more established websites that I subscribe to. I don't access the Internet business websites at all for the same reason. These information sites are primarily there to increase ratings with sensational headlines that feed on our emotions. I strictly limit my market news to the TQQQ chart once daily for 10 minutes. Watching the chart any more frequently will cause you to worry unnecessarily that the price will turn negative as it goes higher or you will miss a daily bottom. Avoid this activity since it causes negative addiction.

We want to maintain a balanced emotional state when approaching the markets. Any emotion one way or the other is detrimental to our financial success. The same is true when reading financial articles about where the markets are headed in the months ahead. Obviously no one can predict where the markets will be months in advance let alone the next day so avoid reading these sensational headlines.

Once you begin to invest as explained above, you will probably want to see and read everything in sight about the market direction since you will be feeling insecure about your decision. Get this out of your system before you commit one dollar to the market. Trade on paper for as long as it takes you to get comfortable with the process then wait some more and continue to read the details in this book. If you see a double bottom or top, go to that page in this book and read it again so that you commit the details to memory. There is no shortcut to familiarity. It comes from reviewing the charts again and again.

What you are doing in reality is repeatedly sticking with the details of what works when watching a stock graph and, therefore, removing the emotion from your buy/sell decision. You need to repeatedly scan the graphs from prior periods. I do this regularly even now since my eye needs to see a frame of reference of graphs from prior periods to remind me of the current period since these prior movements are repeated again and again.

Here are some headlines from the CNBC Internet business website on the same day:

'Watch gold' — Blackstone's Byron Wien teases 2020 market surprises

---

My emotional thought: "Uh-Oh. The market is headed lower! I'd better sell."

DOW PLUNGES 1000 POINTS AS STRETCH OF UNPRECEDENTED VOLATILITY CONTINUES

My emotional thought: "I don't know what to do since the market was up 1000 points yesterday! I'd better sell now. Or maybe not. I don't know."

You get the idea. It is not good to be emotionally whipsawed before you even look at your TQQQ chart. Stay clear of these articles since they will only fill you with excitement or fear. Below we will cover more buy and sell points in graphs to give you more confidence as to the best time to buy and sell.

Here we are at Figure 66 in April 2018 (arrows). No this is not Figure 62 even though they look very similar since Figure 66 is a year later. Patterns are always repeated.

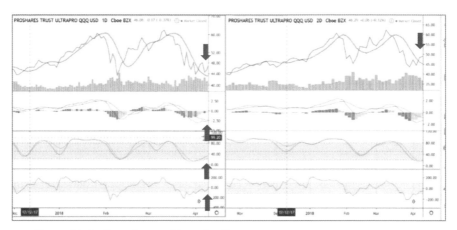

Figure 66: April 2018 – would you buy?

Would you buy or pass? I would buy. Look at the down pointing arrows above. In the graph in this figure the price has moved above the moving average line which is a positive sign. Now look at the upward pointing arrows on the left. Each indicator is moving in an upward direction signaling that the price will go higher. The indicators on the right 2-day graph are also showing signs of moving up even though this graph shows indicator movement a little later than the 1-day.

Here they are again some weeks later (Figure 67) showing that the price did indeed move up. Notice also the large double top in January and March and then the double bottom a little later (brackets).

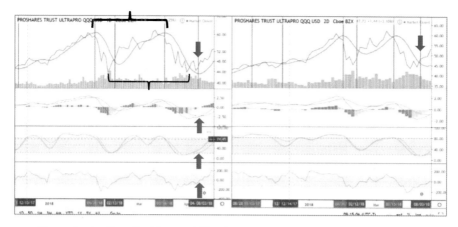

Figure 67: April 2018 – You would buy!

These are strong signs that the price will move higher to hit the prior double top so go for it and buy! You did it, you bought and the price started to rise nicely.

Here we are a few months later (Figure 68) with the same buy point arrows marked as in Figure 66 and 67. Notice the price in the 2-day chart is above the moving average line marked by the arrow.

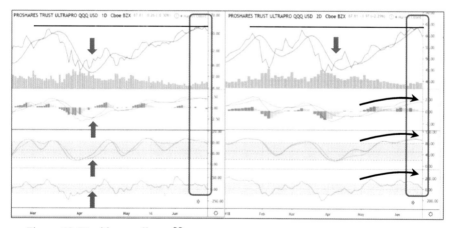

Figure 68: Would you sell now??

Now take a look all the way to the right of each graph marked with a long box. Would you sell? The price in each graph is below the moving average and each indicator in both graphs are starting to turn down. Also, the price did move up to approximately the same point as the double top in Figure 68 as we expected (horizontal lines). Look at the curved arrows on the right graph in Figure 68. Each indicator has shown a smooth arc as the price went higher and the MACD is starting to approach the mid-line to turn negative.

Because of all of the above I would sell. Even though the price had gone up and down on its path higher the indicators in the right graph all showed that there was more positive room to go higher. This is where the 2-day chart is a distinct advantage. It smooths out the choppier movement in the 1-day chart which could have had you buy and sell three times to the one time on the right hand graph during the same period. As a result, the price from 4/9/18 – 6/19/18 went from $45.36 to $63.34 for a +40% gain! Not bad for two months which equates to a +240% gain on an annualized basis.

This example multiplied over nine years and 40 trades is how you could get that whopping percent increase in your initial investment (and using "Compound Investing" to not take profits along the way).

Now look on the right of each graph in Figure 69 which shows the result of your decision to sell. As expected, the price started to drop. You would have sold and locked in your gain. I am glad you sold at the far right since the price dropped -12% from this point.

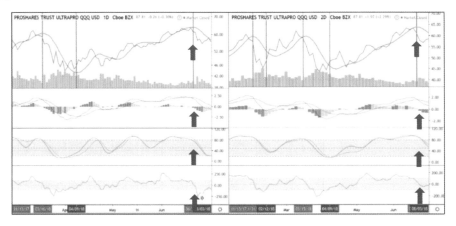

Figure 69: The sell signal shown on the right of each graph

Below in Figure 70 is another double buy/sell (#1 and #2) from July 2017 to November 2017. I have added the vertical lines to show the indicator movement with the price.

In the second buy-sell move (#2) while looking at the 1-day chart you could have bought and sold three times in this one move and no one would have faulted you for being cautious since each downstroke could have ended in disaster. In the right 2-day graph, (#2), notice the MACD indicator then see that the blue line cut below the red line three times, the first time as the move got started, in the middle and again when it was time to sell on the right. On the left graph, the three step move was much clearer and you

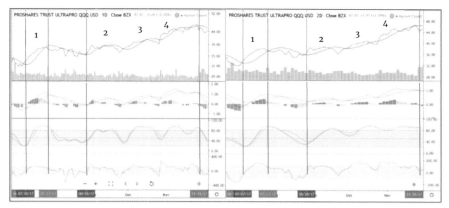

Figure 70: Here is a classic double buy, double sell move. The second move has four sub-moves

would have been justified in selling then buying back three times. If we would have bought and sold four time during this entire period the profit would have been +26% in just four months which is great – let us not get greedy.

These buy-sell situations or setups are repeated over and over so no sense feeling that this is the only time to make money. Even if you weren't paying attention and let one slip by there would be no harm done since the opportunity would present itself about every three months (remember, an average of four to five trades per year in Figure 1a-c).

Below is another one (Figure 71) from an earlier time: June 2016 through June 2017 with four trades during this one year period. Below are three graphs that correspond to each of these four trades (a-d) but enlarged so you can see them more clearly. Each of these four trades is shown below but expanded so it is easier to see.

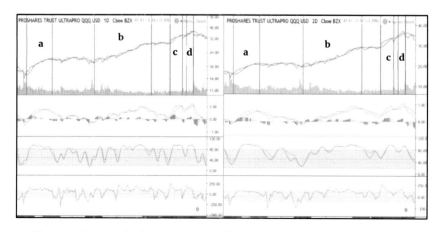

Figure 71: Four trades in a one-year period: June 2016 – June 2017

You can expand each chart yourself by moving the scroll wheel on your mouse forward or back.

In Figure 71: Trade A, see how smooth the arc of the price is which mirrors the smooth arc of each of the indicators. It is most pronounced in the 2-day chart so you would buy it at $16.05 on 6/30/17 and sell at $20.71 on 8/22/16 for an easy +29% profit after just 7 weeks. Notice how all the indicators move smoothly in unison with no jagged movement up or down. These smooth arcing upward moves are the easiest to buy into and the sell signals are very easy to spot represented by the arcing arrows.

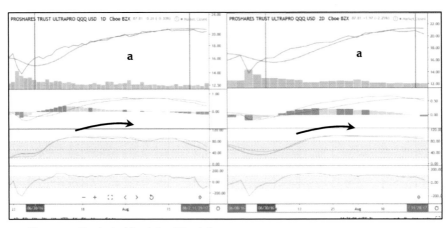

Figure 71: Trade A: 6/30/16 – 8/22/16

Chart 71: Trade B, below, which is the second in the series is almost just as smooth and easy with the buy point at $19.96 on 11/15/16 and the sell price at 28.58 on 3/14/17. The 1-day chart looks choppy but looking at the 2-day chart smooths things out nicely for a profit of +43% in four months.

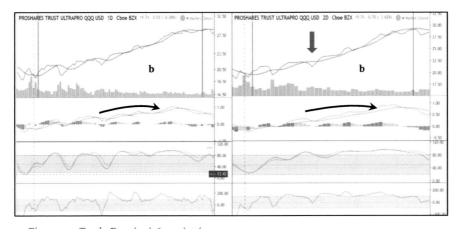

Figure 73: Trade B: 11/15/16 – 3/14/17

There was one point (the downward pointing arrow) that you could have been forgiven for selling then buying back quickly but otherwise, all is smooth. This is the mid-move indicator we discussed earlier but slightly early in the move but, nevertheless, very prominent. On the right hand chart, you can see how easy the sell point is to spot. All indicators clearly start pointing downward. Figure 71: Trade C is just as smooth and easy as Trade A was above. Notice in the 1-day chart how the sell signal is clear but then look at the 2-day chart. It appears that the sell signal is early. That is just the 2-day chart view being a little early.

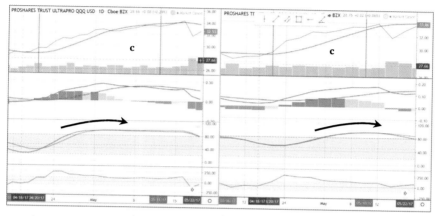

Figure 71: Trade C: 4/21/17 – 5/16/17

This occurred again in Figure 71: Trade D below. This effect doesn't happen often so don't worry about being caught late each time. The 1-day chart will be your guide. Figure 71: Trade D made its move on 5/24/17 at $34.33 and ended two weeks later on 6/8/17 at $37.11 for an +8% gain. Again, notice the smooth arc of the indicators with a clear entry and exit point on the 1-day chart.

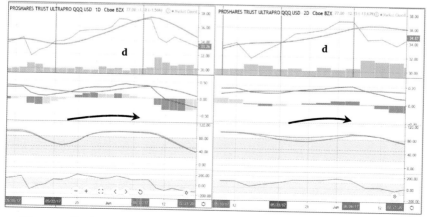

Figure 71: Trade D: 5/24/17 – 6/8/17

SUSTAINED DOWNTRENDS

In Figure 72 below, you will see a sustained downtrend from the sell on 9/5/18 at $68.60 to the next buy point on 1/2/19 at $33.93 for a whopping –51% drop. Notice how I have added a channel as the price dropped. You could have also drawn a downward sloping trendline at the tops of the prices as they moved down for the same effect.

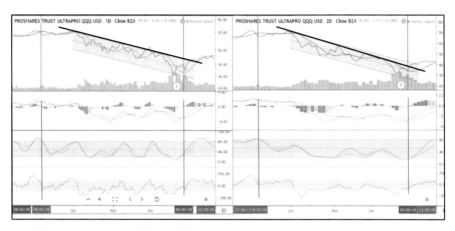

Figure 72: Downtrend from 9/5/18 – 1/2/19

Normally, when the price pops up over the downward sloping trendline is your entry point and, as you can see, all indicators on the 1-day chart on the left were flashing a buy on 1/2/19 which was mirrored on the right hand 2-day chart (right hand green vertical line). The trend line or channel kept you out of the trade while the price was dropping even though there appeared one or two points that would have been fake outs.

As in any price drop like this there are still buyers and sellers but at the micro level day trading so every second of the trading day as well as after-hours buyers and sellers are at it. You are only looking at the bigger picture with one and two day charts so you are out of this short term action keeping your nerves calm.

Take a look at Figure 73 which looks choppy and complicated. At first glance it doesn't look easy to navigate but we are looking at a wide five month view. To make money in this environment you have to zoom in to get a closer look. The good news is that you can zoom in and out quickly and easily with a simple scroll of the mouse. These choppy periods normally occur after one or more big moves up followed by the sideways consolidation period shown here (horizontal lines). The period just proceeding this choppy one produced a +98% return in 6 months! I'll take a +196% return annualized over one year all day long. Why settle for a +1% money market rate or 0.1% in a checking account per year when these returns happen month in and month out. Below is the consolidation period which looks rough. But looking closer this period was made up of four separate moves with a profit large and small. Again remember that you don't know

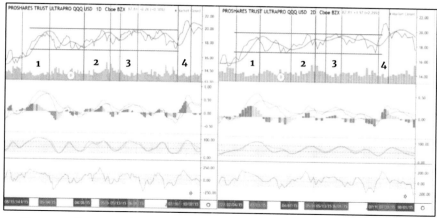

Figure 73: Choppy market from 2/4/15 – 7/23/15

in advance if a move up will be huge, medium, or small. I'll take them all and you may want to also. Notice in this Figure 73 that the sideways price move appears to go nowhere over the entire period on both the 1-day and 2-day charts. In reality, there are four moves up during this sideways period which we will review next.

All together this five month period produced a profit of +43% with four trades so was well worth it. The first zoomed trade is shown in Figure 73: 1st move from 2/4/15 to 3/4/15 or four weeks. So far so good. This trade was pretty easy with a smooth sloping uptrend confirmed by each of the indicators for +17% profit. Zooming in will always show many more trading opportunities than are apparent when we are zoomed out.

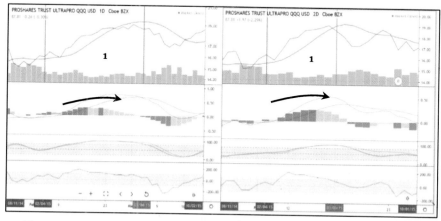

Figure 73: 1st move - Choppy market from 2/4/15 – 3/4/15 +17%

On the next one, Figure 73: 2nd move from 4/8/15 to 5/4/15, I included the period you would have been out of the trade as the price and indicators told you to stay out of the trade during this -5% drop.

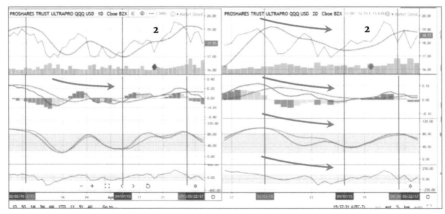

Figure 73: 2nd move − 4/8/15 − 5/4/15 +7%

Again, remember that a -5% drop is not much but suppose it was the beginning of a significant -30% drop?

This can happen at any time so always be on your guard. We want to be in only for the uptrends and not the downtrends so watch your indicators and don't take chances. Always be cautious. This downtrend is very clear on the 2-day chart on the right where you can easily see the indicators on the 2-day chart trending down.

Look at the 1-day chart at the end of the downtrend to see the indicators flashing a buy point (vertical line). Again, on the 2-day chart, the price has moved over the moving average line.

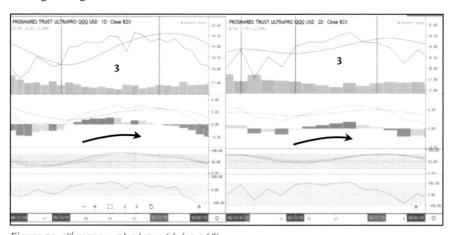

Figure 73: 3rd move − 5/13/15 − 6/1/15 +6%

Figure 73 shows the 3rd move of this set. This move was as smooth as the prior ones with a +6% gain. After a while you may say to yourself why should I go to this trouble for a +6% gain? Remember two points, first, only a +6% gain in two weeks translates to a +156% gain annualized, second, if the uptrend was sustained it could have easily been a +45% gain. If, at this point in your journey your balance was $150,000, this one +6% gain would have been $9,000! I'll take that all day.

You never know how long or short the uptrend will be which is why it is smart to not miss any uptrends. Take them all since they come along like the next passenger train according to a regular schedule on average of four or five times per year.

See Figure 73: 4th move of the series. I don't have to draw curved arrows or vertical lines for you to see the entry and exit points clearly. Again, as in the above paragraph, this trade did better than the +6% gain for a +13% gain so you never know what is around the next corner for you to make big money. Again, 13% of that $150,000 trading balance is $19,500 for this one trade of many vs $550 for a money market account at 0.37% per year!

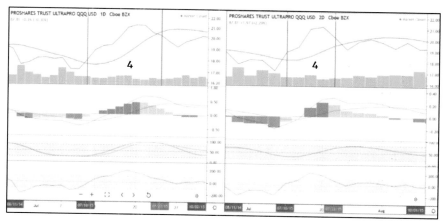

Figure 73: 4th move − 7/10/15 − 7/23/15 +13%

Altogether, these four moves over five months produced a +43% gain which is a +103% gain annualized. You don't have to settle for the miniscule interest rate PER YEAR on a money market account when you can make this kind of money with minimal effort just checking the charts online once a day for 10 minutes over lunch.

Let's look at the next example which occurred recently starting 1/2/18 and ending on 1/24/20 or just about two years for a gain of +179%. Figure 74 shows a portion of this gain from 10/17/18 to 1/24/20 which shows the four uptrends after the significant drop in price. As is usually the case, this giant move up was proceeded by a giant move down from 10/4/18 at $67.28 to 12/24/18 at $30.39 for a total drop of -55%. We want to pay attention to prevent this disaster from occurring since it took almost thirteen months for the price to move from $37.57 on 9/14/17 to $71.55 on 10/1/18 and only three months for the price to go back to $37.57 on 1/2/19 so the down move took only 25% of the time to drop as it took to rise.

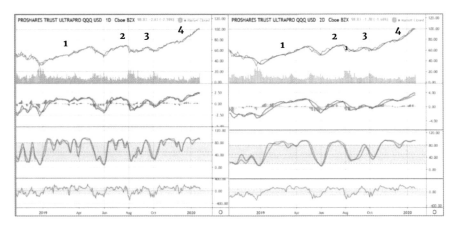

Figure 74: See the 1-day/2-day chart from 1/2/2018 to 1/24/20

Let's take a closer look at these individual moves by zooming in to see each separate move in more detail. This first move (Figure 74: 1st move) started on 1/2/18 at $37.57 and ended on 5/1/19 at $65.33 for +74%. Notice the arrow at the mid-move indicator which was the exact mid-point of the move which registered on the 1-day and 2-day charts and also see the trendline I drew (dotted line) which marked the steady move higher with no downward movement along the way. The arcs of the MACD are also rising smoothly on the 2-day chart.

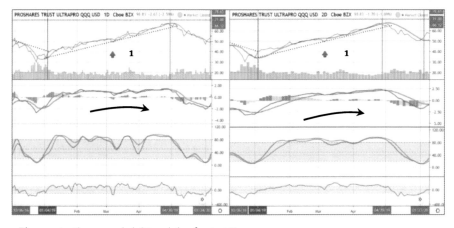

Figure 74: 1st move: 1/2/18 to 5/1/19 for +74%

After this four month move up there followed a five week move down for a drop of -29%. As I said earlier, after a large move up there follows a dramatic move down in a fraction of the time so be prepared for these drops. The next move up is shown in Figure 74: 2nd move from 6/5/19 at $51.94 to 7/25/19 at $68.05 or +31%.

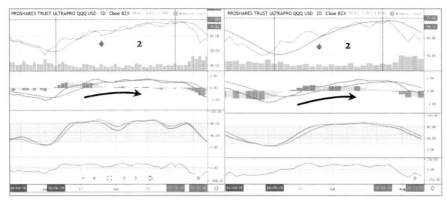

Figure 74: 2nd move: 6/5/19 to 7/25/19 for +31%

On the 2-day chart, see the smooth upward arc of the MACD and the arrow at the mid-move indicator which was close to the mid-point of the move and registered on the 1-day chart but not on the 2-day chart. Now there followed a drop of -18% followed by the next move up, Figure 74: 3rd going up from 8/27/19 at $58.27 to 9/19/19 at $65.48 for +12%.

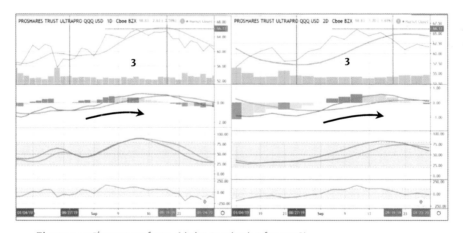

Figure 74: 3rd move up from 6/5/19 to 7/25/19 for +12%

Before this last big move up there was a drop of -9%. What followed next was the last big move of this period starting on 10/10/19 at $61.15 and ending on 1/24/20 at $98.83 for a +62% gain in Figure 74: 4th. See the mid-move indicator again. Also, I drew the first trendline (dotted line) as the price moved up and then drew a second trendline at a higher angle than the first which marked the climax top.

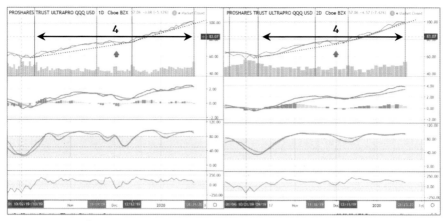

Figure 74: 4th move up from 10/10/19 to 1/24/20 for +62%

Since the drop at the mid-move indicator was more significant than prior ones and registered on both charts I broke this one move into two moves up. Since the indictors were flashing a sell at the mid-move, I prudently sold then bought back two weeks later with no loss.

If you see your indicators flashing a sell signal don't hesitate to sell then buy back if the upward trend continues. You may miss a few dollars buying back at a slightly higher price but that is ok since you do not want to hold at the start of a significant drop. At this point I bought back and the move up continued significantly higher.

Normally, you want to sell then buy back at a somewhat lower price as a move ends but sometimes this doesn't work out and you may be forced to buy back at a slightly higher price. Don't worry too much about this. Your overall gains will far outweigh these small losses.

SIGNIFICANT MARKET CORRECTIONS (> -10%)

In the following pages we will review numerous more examples of buy and sell decisions from previous time frames both good and bad but more challenging so you can feel more confident. I will also include examples from prior market crashes so you can be familiar with what to do and what to watch out for. I'm presenting these case studies so you can use them as examples of the many similar situations that you will encounter. The only way to overcome future challenges is to have examples from the past as your guide. Since TQQQ starting posting daily results on Feb. 2010 some of the examples will be for the NASDAQ 100 prior to this date. Since we are using the NASDAQ 100 instead of TQQQ all percent gains will be multiplied by three.

1987: The first example is from the market crash of 1987 including the days leading up to this event (Figure 75). Looking at the chart all was proceeding normally since we were not listening to or reading the headlines during this time (as soon as we

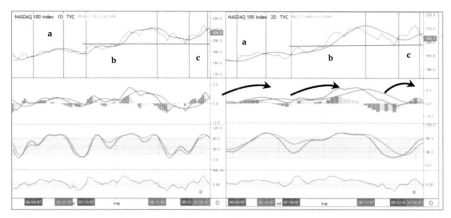

Figure 75: Four months from 6/4/87 to 10/7/87 leading up to the 1987 market crash

read or hear something negative, our adrenaline will start pumping and we will be in fear). At "a" we entered the trade on 6/4/87 at $186.40 and exited this trade on 6/26/87 at $191.10 for a gain of +8% (3 x +2.6%) in 17 trading days.

The next trade (b) presented itself seven trading day later on 7/3/87 at $190.40 and went to 8/31/87 for a gain of +30% (3 x +10%) in 40 trading days. During these 40 days we were watching the charts for only 10 minutes each day to make sure all was on track. The price then moved below the moving average on both charts and our indicators were turning negative indicating a reversal was coming. Remember, we never know how small or large the next move will be so we want to capture each move and always need to be vigilant for dramatic moves up or down since we never know when they will occur.

The last move of this group (c) started on 9/23/87 at $204.10 and ended on 10/7/87 at $206.90 for a profit of +4% (3 x +1.4%). These three moves netted us +42% in four months or +122% annualized. For each move see the three smooth arcs on the MACD indicator in the 2-day chart. On 10/7/87 we were safely out of our trades waiting for the next one to come along just like waiting at the station for the next train to come and with the same regularity. These three trades were somewhat choppier but nevertheless just as profitable. The next move was when the market collapsed a few days after we safely exited the trade on 10/7/87 at the right of "c". The black horizontal line indicates support & resistance since the resistance is at the left of "b" preventing the price from moving higher and the support is at the left of "c" preventing the price from going lower. Once this support was broken to the downside on the far right of the charts (not shown), the price would most probably continue lower. You can apply this principle to most uptrends and downtrends where finding support and resistance is to your advantage.

A few days later the price dropped from $206.90 to $128.40 for a -114% drop (3 X -38%) confirming our expectations. As discussed, these drops are fast and sudden and we don't know where the bottom will end. The above support/resistance line once broken would be our clue to enter the trade with SQQQ. The following –114% drop in TQQQ (Figure 76) would have seen a corresponding gain of +114% in less than three weeks! This is the power of the T's and S's. There were some clues we could find if we looked.

For example, there was a small attempt to recover at the arrow which failed. The price then climbed above the moving average on both charts. With a big drop of this magnitude we always have to be aware of the possibility that the price will go lower so this small jump could have been another fake out prior to the next drop down so we waited.

The price then did go down (Figure 76) to the prior low or support (lower horizontal line) and then turned up after approximately five week of waiting. This was our signal (1) to safely enter the trade at $139.80 on 12/9/87 and exit again on 1/12/88 at $155.70 for a +33% gain (3 X +11%) in about 4 weeks. It finally took 24 months for the price to get back to the high on 10/7/87. Going forward, I will dispense with the x3 calculation and only list the final percent as if we were trading TQQQ.

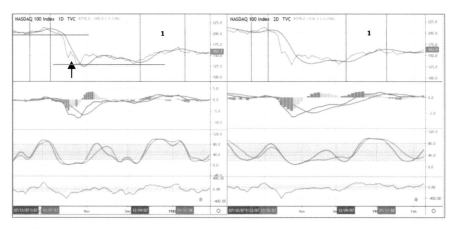

Figure 76: The results of the crash from 10/7/87 to 12/9/87 and beyond

In those 24 months, we would have had many more trades for significant gains which would have been missed if we didn't know what we were doing and rode the drop all the way down. Since a market correction is generally considered a drop of –10% or more, we will review a few more that were greater than this even though they weren't considered a "crash". Since I've only reviewed moves up in the prior pages, I'm reviewing these moves down to show you that they do occur with some frequency and to be always on the lookout for them. They may not occur with the frequency of the moves up but can and do negate many of our prior gains if we are not always looking out for them. In the last ten years I have mentioned that the market bias is up so we could become complacent and believe that this bias will continue forever. This attitude breeds laziness and will lead to losses.

1990: The next significant move down occurred from 7/13/90 to 10/10/90 with a drop from $244.70 to $165.20 of -96%. The leadup to the drop is shown in Figure 77. The buy price on 5/2/90 was $208.50 and the sell price on 6/8/90 was $234.70 for a TQQQ gain of +39% in about six weeks. As you can see, all of these "routine" gains are significant and your percent gain and dollar gain are increasing exponentially with "Compound Investing". Doesn't this chart from 1990 look almost identical to Figure 75 leading up to the 1987 market crash? You will see this phenomenon repeated again and again and is human nature at work. Just to the right of each chart all indicators were flashing SELL in unison especially the MACD in the 2-day chart pointing down.

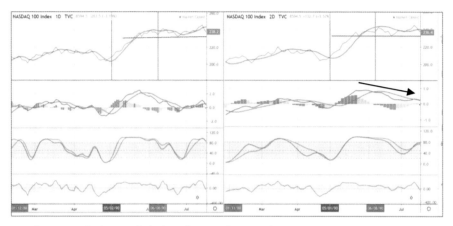

Figure 77: The last trade before the next drop: 5/1/90 to 6/6/90

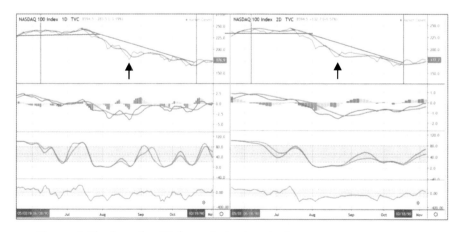

Figure 78: The drop of -96% from 7/13/90 to 10/10/90

We had no time to catch our breath at the end of the above trade when the floor fell away and we entered another big drop of -96% from July 1990 to October 1990 (Figure 78) with a corresponding gain of +96% by switching from TQQQ to SQQQ.

There was a fake out at the arrows which barely registered on the 2-day chart. If you entered the trade at the arrow thinking it was the end of the down trend, you would have exited quickly as the price dropped below the moving average. You have to be vigilant with these huge drops since they continue downward in steps as explained earlier. We drew a trendline which, "surprisingly", ended at the next buy point. This is another indicator that was explained earlier.

Trendlines and channels can be used regularly. Now, let's remember, this was 1990, thirty years ago showing all the same chart patterns as today. What phenomenal gains were in store for us in the following thirty years? This is why you will become a millionaire following these tried and true techniques for success.

What immediately followed the above drop were two gains from 10/26/90 to 12/25/90 for +50% and from 1/15/91 to 4/17/91 for +111% or +166% in 5 months. These double and triple digit gains will line up for you like dominoes ready for you to grab again and again. You just have to know ahead of time that they will return like the day follows the night.

2000: What followed next were ten years of phenomenal gains until the dot-com crash (Figure 79). Up to this time there were no crashes with the magnitude of this one since 1929 which led to the great depression. This drop went from $4691.60 to $815.40 for a **-248% drop** if trading TQQQ.

If we traded SQQQ as these drops unfolded our profit would have been +249%. This drop had five distinct steps, 1-5, identical to Figure 48. Again, repeating patterns over the years representing human nature. All the way down there were five trades (1-5) to be made prudently but clearly since we were in a long term drop which I just started magnifying for you. The double and triple tops and bottoms do not have to align exactly

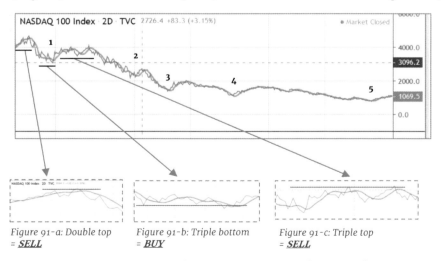

Figure 91-a: Double top = **_SELL_**

Figure 91-b: Triple bottom = **_BUY_**

Figure 91-c: Triple top = **_SELL_**

Figure 79: The dot.com crash from 3/23/00 to 10/3/02 for a drop of -248%

to be called double and triple tops and bottoms. In your charting program you can view these for yourself and finish identifying the remainder as a good exercise in conditioning your eyes to PROFITS!

2008: Now, here we were eight years later facing the same drop (Figure 80). But, you would have been ready with your arsenal of techniques and would have seen this one coming a mile away. Since you were constantly vigilant for the next upswing and downswing you would have anticipated being out of the market ahead of this big one again. I am not going to itemize each trade but will identify each significant milestone on the way down that you should be able to identify by now for yourself.

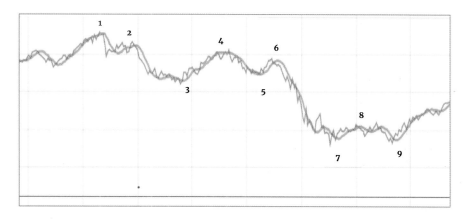

Figure 80: The financial crisis of 2008 for a drop of -162%

Here was each trade amid the drops:

- At the top at #1 you would have been safely out of the trade since your indicators were clearly flashing a sell while netting you a profit of +45%.

- We bought back when the price moved above the moving average then sold at Trade #2 were there was a double top which was clearly a sell signal netting you +12%.

- We waited as the price continued to drop until the entry point at #3 where, again, the price popped above the moving average and the sell at #4 for a gain of +42%.

- Another buy showed itself at #5 and we sold at #6 for a gain of +15%.

- Then we entered the next trade at #7 with an out at #8 with a net of +30%.

- Finally, we entered the next trade at #9 which was ongoing in this chart. Also notice the double bottom between #7 and #9 as further corroboration the this was the bottom of the downtrend.

We turned this tremendous drop of -162% into a gain of +144% in five trades. How did we accomplish this magic act of turning lead to gold like an alchemist? Here were the steps to unravel the mystery:

- We totally disregarded the news that was blasting SELL, SELL, SELL with no bottom. How crazy. As we know, there always is a bottom so we just watched and waited while making money along the way.

- We only focused on our indicators to show us the way. They continually flashed buy, then sell, then buy, then sell, again and again. We just did what they told us to do with no magic.

- We remained 100% focused on the 1-day/2-day charts which never failed us.

- We reviewed past downturns which were a repeat of our current downturn and showed numerous repeating patterns of double and triple tops, double and triple bottoms, trendlines, support, and resistance zones.

The only way to use the above techniques to make these amazing profits is to study, study, study, then go back at least ten years and work your way forward to the present and review each buy and sell setup until you thoroughly know and can recognize each pattern and tool that I have reviewed. I made this journey and continue to go back to prior times to get my eyes accustomed to the current situation and how it mirrors the past. There is no magic, just work, as you would planning a new job or a trip to another country or setting up a retirement plan at age 25. You need to be this far sighted to make this kind of money regularly. It is totally doable as I have shown you again and again in these pages and as I have done myself.

In a sense I look forward to these drops since they make way for unlimited future opportunities to make big money in the stock market with swing trades. As per prior drops of this magnitude there will be plateaus where the price will pause on the way down that will be entry points for more trades as in Figure 80.

CLIMAX TOPS

I mentioned climax tops much earlier and we see two in action in Figures 81 and 82 below. A climax top is when the price is increasing over time until, suddenly, the price takes on a much steeper incline and ends in a much shorter time.

In Figure 81, the uptrend started on 8/28/17 and continued for four months to 12/29/17 with an appreciation of +28%. Suddenly, the price accelerated upwards and ended one month later on 1/25/18 with an additional appreciation of +31%. There followed a significant drop of -25% in two weeks.

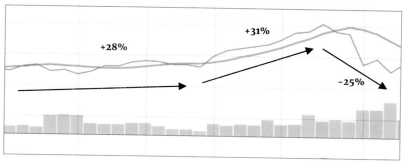

Figure 81 : Climax top 12/29/17 − 1/25/18

Notice how the price moved below the moving average in each case to signal a sell. Missing these sell signals would prove very costly especially during a climax top.

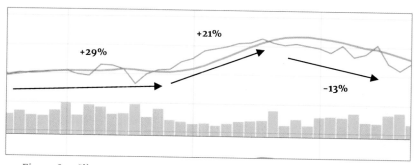

Figure 82 : Climax top 5/17/13 to 6/19/13

Figure 82 shows another climax top. This upward move started on 11/16/12 until 4/25/13 for 5 months, and an appreciation of +29%. Suddenly, the price jumped at an elevated incline to top out on 5/17/13 for another increase of +21% in three weeks! The price then dropped for 4 weeks for a decrease of -13%.

Climax tops don't occur often but when they do there is plenty of money to be made in a very short time compared with the preceding up move. But be careful since climax tops are almost always followed by a sudden and significant drop in a very short time so watch your indicators closely.

To illustrate that this is not confined to TQQQ, Figure 83 shows the stock, Tesla, during a climax top as an example only. Since TESLA is included in the NASDAQ 100 it will exhibit similar price changes as TQQQ. This is very graphically shown as the price dropped for a loss of -10% then suddenly started climbing gradually then really accelerated at an incline for a gain of +56%.

Again, stick with TQQQ since adding individual stocks adds a significant element of uncertainty and risk. This chart shows how unpredictable an individual stock can be.

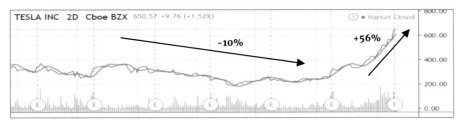

Figure 83: Climax top for Tesla 10/25/19 to 1/27/20

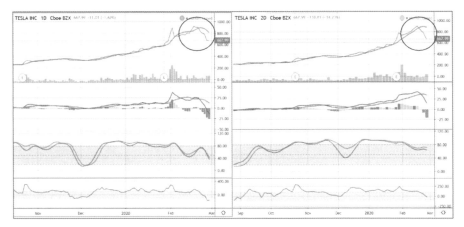

Figure 84: Climax top for Tesla 1/27/20 to 2/28/20

In Figure 84, the price continued to climb from $650.57 in the above chart to $917.42, or +41% in 14 trading days. See how quickly the profits added up but the drop would surely come which can be seen where the price dropped to $667.99 or -$27% in 7 trading days. As of this writing the downtrend has just begun so who knows where this will end (not happily I am sure).

The next market crash also qualifies as a climax top. In Figure 85 the price gyrated up and down from Feb 2018 to Oct 2019 with the price not moving up or down significantly until suddenly the price started shooting upwards. We want to occasionally zoom out for a 1-2 year view to see this characteristic then zoom back in to your normal view.

2020: As I am now writing, we are in the midst of a classic crash called the Coronavirus crash which is occurring at the same time as an oil price crash (Figure 85). The reason for the crash and the headlines documenting the crash will be lost to history in a few years but the drop will be remembered as a classic case of a climax top whatever the reason as shown on the chart below. I will identify every up move in chronologic order starting on 4/6/18 (1) through 2/20/20 (14). The climax top is clearly shown with the arrow at a steep angle to the rest of the chart and the drop is shown with the bold vertical arrow.

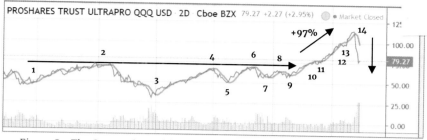

Figure 85: The Coronavirus crisis of 2020 for a drop of -36% and starting

This chart is for a two-year period and is compressed so may be hard to see on this chart but just put in the dates below on your own charting program and follow along:

1. Double bottom on 4/6/18: entry price $44.47.

2. Double top on 10/3/18: exit price $71.35. _Profit **+60%**._

3. "V" price formation on 12/24/18: entry price $30.39.

4. Double top on 5/3/19: exit price $67.57. _Profit **+122%**._

5. "V" price formation on 6/3/19: entry price $47.01

6. Triple top on 7/26/19: exit price $70.07. _Profit **+49%**._

7. Triple bottom on 8/23/19: entry price $55.78

8. Price moves sideways on 9/19/19: exit price $65.48. _Profit **+17%**._

9. Double bottom on 10/8/19: entry price $58.08.

10. Price below M.A. on 11/20/19: exit price $74.58. _Profit **+28%**._

11. Price above M.A. on 12/11/19: entry price $77.38.

12. Price below M.A. on 1/24/19: exit price $98.83. _Profit **+28%**._

13. Double bottom on 1/31/19: entry price 93.64.

14. Price below M.A. on 2/20/20: exit price $114.70. _Profit **+23%**._

We were out at this point when the price dropped to $75.82 for a percent change of **-51% in one week**. All we did was watch our indicators and how the price moved within the indicators to buy when we were told to and sell when we were told to by our price and indicators. During this sixteen month period we accrued a phenomenal profit of **+327%** with no losses!

As the months progressed the buy and sell points became more and more compressed as, at the same time, the price started to escalate higher and higher at an unsustainable angle. Prior to this escalation the price movement was essentially flat (horizontal arrow) then suddenly started taking off. These are the hallmarks of a climax top leading to a sudden and severe drop. The actual reason for the sudden drop is not important since the market was looking for any reason to sell, no matter how important or unimportant since this price action could not continue to go on at this pace. As of this writing the price is at $37.25 on 3/16/20 (blue dotted line in Figure 86) so it took three weeks to undo an uptrend that started 32 months ago for a current drop of -68%! We will see where the bottom will be but my guess is at either $30.39 on 12/24/18 or $20.71 on 12/3/15. During this drop there will be numerous entry and exit points for significant profits like all the prior crashes in the past so don't fret. There will be endless opportunities in the future.

Looking at Figure 86, as the climax top made way for a market crash, there were plenty of support and resistance lines to estimate where the bottom would be from the past. Again, the past is constantly repeated in the present. All we have to do is look back to see what will happen in the future.

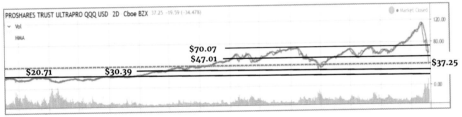

Figure 86: Future support levels for the bottom of this crash

LINE, BAR, HEIKEN ASHI OR CANDLESTICK CHART FOR PRICE

There are a few ways to view the price line in your chart such as: bar, line, candlestick, hollow candlestick, area, Heiken Ashi, and Renko to name a few. In your online research you will probably see each chart using the bar or candlestick to represent the price. I have used the line to represent the price in all the charts in this book since, I believe, the movement of the price is easier to see as it moves above and below the moving average line. This is something I have conditioned my eyes to see. You can experiment with these different choices to suite your own style. Each graphing program has the capability to quickly change the price view to these other choices at the touch of a button so try each one. I am describing each price style in an extremely brief way so do some research for an expanded description of each style on your own.

The following figures will illustrate my point. Figure 87 has the price shown as a candlestick. The candlestick view shows the price movement for each day as a colored box, green for up and red for down. The height of each box shows the price movement for each day, so a long box represents a large daily price movement and vice versa. As you can see, the price appears much choppier with each passing day so each day's price appears somewhat disjointed from the others.

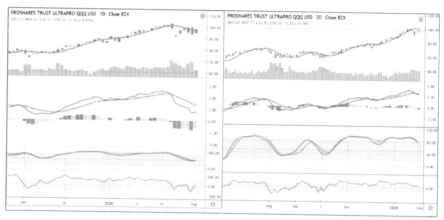

Figure 87: The daily price represented as a candle

In Figure 88, another candle chart called the Heiken Ashi candle averages the current day's closing price with the prior day's closing price to create a box that is the average of the two days. As a result, the price is an average and not the actual price for that day. The main advantage of this candle style is that an extended trend is easier to see and stay with since the price is less choppy above and below the moving average and the red and green price boxes appear to stay with the trend for a longer time. The price of the candle at the extreme right is $96.64 but the actual price is $97.79 so there is some discrepancy between these two prices.

Major drops are not reversed in days as most investors would like but in weeks and months as is true in reality. Again, the entry point on 2/12/19 in Figure 89 coincided with the price moving up to the top of the downward pointing channel on the 1-day chart, the Heiken Ashi bar turning green on the 2-day chart, and the MACD turning green also on the 2-day chart. We need these multiple confirmations to feel confident of the entry point or we will be whipsawed again and again for continuing losses. Consider all these arrows in your arsenal and don't discount any of them without your own back testing to prove to yourself that something just doesn't work and you can discount it.

The main advantage explained above also comes in handy when considering reentering the trade after a big drop such as following a market crash or major correction such as occurred on 2/20/20. The Heiken Ashi bars will remain in the red on the 2-day chart since it is averaging the prior two days.

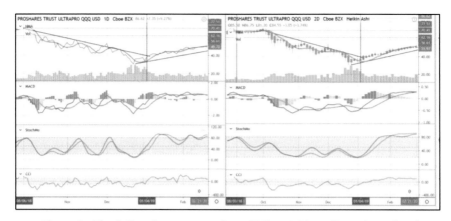

Figure 89: The daily price represented as a Heiken Ashi candle on the 2-day chart showed a drop of -40% in 3 months.

When the bar turns green it is signaling that the last two days were from a positive price or one down day and a large up day so that the two average to a green positive bar. Of course we must also use other tools to verify a bottom such as a trend line or channel since there will be fake outs to the upside only to continue the trend down.

In Figure 89 we sold on the extreme left on the 2-day chart on 9/5/18 at $68.60 then watched the chart show a massive selloff until 1/8/19 for four months. We used a trendline to touch the top of each price as it jumped up in an attempted fake out but continued lower. The chart attempted to rally twice on the way down yet the trendline was not broken. Finally, the price moved up a third time touching the trendline while, at the same time, the 1-day MACD was in green territory and the Heiken Ashi bar also turned green. This was our signal to reenter for the start of the next trade. This drop

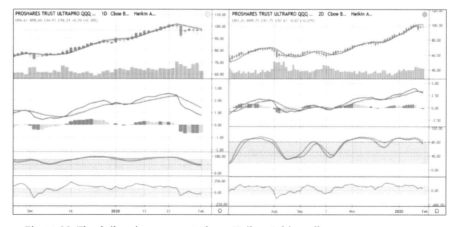

Figure 88: The daily price represented as a Heiken Ashi candle

completed for a loss of -41%. This rule of three's is repeated again and again on the way up and on the way down so add this to your arsenal for future trades.

In any event even with the Heiken Ashi the first green bar still needs to be at or over the moving average on the 2-day chart. The following examples will illustrate two bottoms and two tops. One trick I have learned with the Heiken Ashi bar on the 1-day chart is my "Rule of Many Days". This rule states that at the bottom of a move down and at the top of a move up, there are five to seven days where the Heinken Ashi bars move sideways on the 1-day chart as a signal that the reversal is immenent. Start counting from the first green bar above the moving average.

"RULE OF MANY DAYS"

You can see it in Figure 90 below. The first green bar was on 12/27/18 followed by five days of the Heiken Ashi bars going sideways. Notice all the indicators moving up at the same time. The fifth day was the buy day. Here it is again but on the sixth day, Figure 91. Again, all indicators are moving up in unisen.

Here it is again at a top starting on 7/17/19 in Figure 92. The sell day was followed by a -7% drop a few days later. Better be a little early with all indicators dropping than late and losing money.

Be careful since sometime this rule does not work as in Figure 93. Here we saw a "V" shaped bottom which are not that common where the first green bar is rather large then the price started to immediately move up. In this case, the second green bar would have been the buy price.

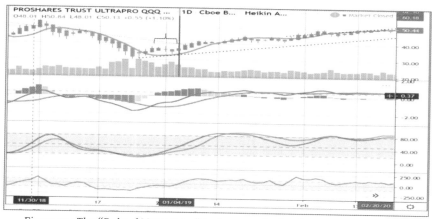

Figure 90: The "Rule of Many Days" is shown at the bracket on the 1-day chart 12/27/18.

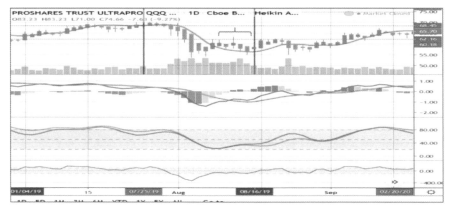

Figure 91: The "Rule of Many Day" is shown at the bracket on the 1-day chart with the buy date of 8/16/19.

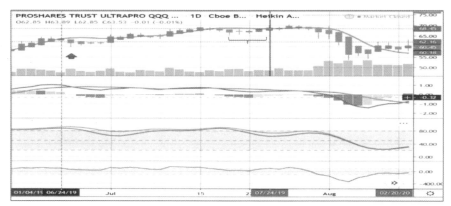

Figure 92: The "Rule of Many Days" is shown at the bracket on the 1-day chart 7/24/19.

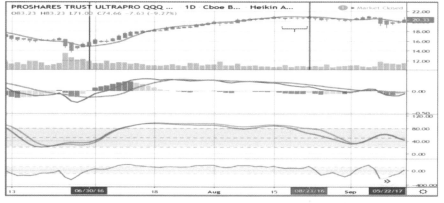

Figure 93: The "Rule of Many Days" does not work here in the 1-day chart with a buy date on 6/29/16.

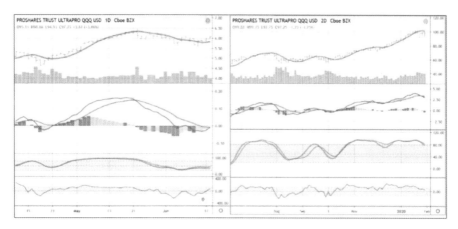

Figure 94: The daily price represented as a bar

Figure 94 shows a chart with the price as a bar with the green bar for a price rise and a red bar for a price drop. Looking closely, the bar will show the opening price, the high for the day, the low for the day, and the closing price for the day. For me this is information that I don't necessarily need so it adds to the complexity of my trading. For me the bar is a little harder to see compared to a line. Remember, simple is better.

When researching online charts the price bar and the price candlestick will be the most common representation of the price you will see. That doesn't necessarily mean that these styles are better or worse than any other. Use the style that works best for you.

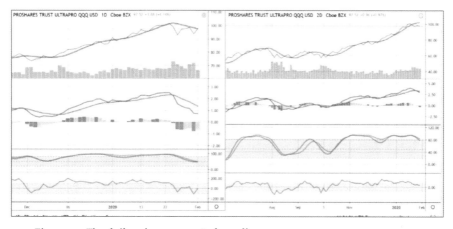

Figure 95: The daily price represented as a line

Above, Figure 95, is the same view of the price as a line,. Each view can be changed with a click of a button. Traders use each one for different reasons but most stay with one because they started trading with that one and their eyes got accustomed to using that one. You decide which one is the simplest and easiest to see and use.

Another technique I use regularly besides comparing the 1-day chart to the 2-day chart is to compare the 2-day charts of TQQQ to SQQQ next to one another. You can do this easily in TradingView with a few key strokes (Figure 96).

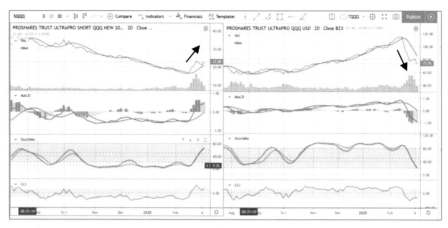

Figure 96: Compare SQQQ to TQQQ in the same screen.

The SQQQ will be a mirror image of TQQQ with the reverse price. Here TQQQ was down -8.5% while SQQQ was up +8.5%. I use this technique to ask myself if I would buy SQQQ if TQQQ was getting ready to drop and vice versa. It brings a fresh view to my buy/sell decisions. In this figure TQQQ was really taking a beating as was the whole market in Feb-March 2020 so I sold TQQQ on 2/21/20 at $108.14 and at the same time bought SQQQ for $17.39. As of this writing TQQQ is at $39.31 for a drop of -64% and SQQQ is up at $26.94 for a gain of +55%. Not bad for 2 weeks of investing.

SUMMARY POINTS:

- **Emotion most definitely enters into buy/sell decisions. Avoid reading online stock sources with scare headlines that may influence you to buy or sell.**

- **Buy and sell decisions are readily apparent only after you have been studying for some time so practice and practice some more with your paper trades.**

- **Always look to the 2-day chart for confirmation before committing to the buy or sell.**

- Timeframes can be long or short. Very short intraday timeframes are for day traders and very long ones are for buy-and-hold investors. A one week timeframe will get you in and out of a trade too late resulting in reduced profits. Use the 1-day and 2-day chart timeframes to view price movement that is most accurate for four to five trades per year where you will capture virtually all upward moves.

CHAPTER SEVEN

Money Management and Risk

So far we have reviewed the nuts and bolts of trading TQQQ in good times and bad. We have come quite a way from minimal knowledge of the stock market to making money regularly and consistently with significantly lower risk. I mentioned earlier that I had started with $3,000, got a brokerage account, set up a trading platform, focused on the ETF TQQQ to the exclusion of all other investments to keep it simple, then practiced for a long time while I learned to recognize buy and sell signals. After I felt more comfortable, I started investing the $3,000 in early trades leveraging the gains thru "Compound Investing" and without taking any profits to a significant balance that I thought I'd never reach. It just took consistency, focus, and paying attention each day for the next opportunity to show itself. All I was really doing was watching what everyone else was doing and then just following along using my charts as a window into the investment community. Each buy and sell signal was there in my face and all I had to do was act on the signals. All along the way I kept it simple with just four indicators and the price line to tell me the next move. I had to stay focused since I didn't know when the next buy day would come along. It could have been in a day, week or many weeks but I had to stay focused each day. If I got bored and stopped watching the charts each day the next buying opportunity would pass me by. I was determined to not let any of these opportunities slip by me.

You can do the same. Start with the basics by reading this book in its entirety. Read along with your charting program open and in front of you on the date shown on each chart. See if you see what I saw and explained. Do that for every chart in the book.

There is a temptation when opening your brokerage account and depositing that first amount of money you will invest to also choose a margin account. Don't do this. A margin account lets you borrow a certain percent of your capital so you can invest with a larger amount of money. If you happen to have some losses in your first trading experiments you will owe on that borrowed money the amount that you lost plus the interest since the brokerage house charges you higher than normal interest on the borrowed money being about 10% on trading funds under $10,000.

Start with an amount of money you can afford to absolutely do without. That is right, an amount that you don't need or extra money you won't miss. This is money you don't need in the next few months to pay bills with or that you will need for an emergency. It could be hundreds or thousands.

You can build your confidence by starting with a smaller amount and gradually increase it as you get more comfortable with the process. With this small amount of money it may seem like it will take forever for your dollar gains to start accumulating. Don't worry about this, only focus on the percent gains to judge your success or failure not your dollar gains. if you focus on your dollar gains, you will be motivated to take bigger risks which could backfire. If you maintain a positive percent gain however small or large with each trade your confidence will grow and the percent appreciation will accumulate translating into your dollar gain growing. Once you are totally comfortable with the principles in this book you won't necessarily lose money but you don't want to start trading with money that you will need. The reason for this is that you will be able to invest without pressure to perform to a certain self-created standard like "I have got to make a profit equal to my mortgage each month". This is a self-defeating way to start and you will undoubtably fail. In this mind set you will be checking your chart numerous times a day and second guessing your buy and sell decision. You will sell when you should stay in the trade or you may enter into a high risk entry point even though, in hindsight, you should have known better.

Don't lose sight of your risk tolerance or how much risk you feel comfortable with. If you are about to make that first buy, check in with yourself and see if you are especially nervous. This may be a clue that a) you are not ready to take the plunge or b) the buy point may not be checking off all the boxes, namely:

1. Price below the moving average
2. The 2-day chart not aligned with the 1-day chart
3. The three lower indicators not flashing a buy signal in unison

If any of the above are showing, don't make the trade. A bad trade will not become a good trade by magic. You have to plan a good trade in advance and see it coming before it is there which is called "the setup". If you can make a few good trades in a row, your confidence will grow exponentially. Don't forget about the sell side of the equation. If you made a good buy a day will come when you have to sell. Don't go by my averages in the beginning table above. These numbers are just averages (4.5 trades/month; average hold days=53; average days between trades=37). The actual numbers may be very different for you so stay open to change.

Occasionally, you may have a loss. Accept this before starting. If you always think you will only have gains you are not being realistic. Now I'm not saying that you will have losses, but accept the reality that you may. With enough practice you can absolutely avoid losses but you have to be prepared. Mark up your charting program as I have done in the above figures with green buy and red sell lines and go back ten years and work your way to the present. You will have enough examples to get used to most situations. In fact, each situation will be repeated again and again. Remember that the market represents human nature and human nature doesn't change so what happened ten years ago will be repeated tomorrow.

Keep your head out of the financial websites. Everything you need to know for success is right there in the charts. There are no new secrets or answers that will make you go from losing to winning. Reread this book as many times as is necessary and follow along in your charting program using the 1-day/2-day charts. All your answers will be right there in front of your eyes.

Another temptation you may have is to invest in other types of ETFs and take bigger chances to increase your dollar balance. Don't do it. This will just be a diversion and increase your chances of failure. If you know your one ETF intimately, namely TQQQ, your chances of success will skyrocket. Each stock, ETF, or any other type of investment has its own "personality". It may be volatile, sedate, or in between. I believe TQQQ is relatively sedate in combination with the indicators I have shown you so that the risks are significantly reduced. With this ETF there are no quarterly earnings surprises as with common stocks. There are no surprises as when a CEO suddenly quits his job. These events can cause significant fluctuation in the daily price of a stock that are beyond your indicators to predict. With TQQQ there are no surprises. Most "surprises" such as a Fed interest rate increase or decrease are already factored into the market so really there are no new surprises. Even ignoring dramatic national headlines like an overseas conflict can be seen ahead of time on the charts. Suddenly, your charts will weaken and start trading sideways. Without even knowing what is happening in the world you will already be prepared to sell. It still amazes me that this is how it works. The charts are all you need and they tell all.

With every action in life, whether on a daily basis or contemplating that next big job opportunity and the corresponding move to another state, it is your job to minimize the risk. By investing in TQQQ the risk is very low as compared to that new job. Take a look at the next two lists for a comparison.

NEW JOB RISKS:
- Do I have what it takes to succeed?
- Do they see something in me that I don't see in myself?
- How much responsibility will I be given that I don't know about today?
- What is the personality of my new boss and will we clash?
- How will I get along with my new coworkers?
- How will my family adjust to a move to a new state?
- How will I find the best new school for my kids and will they adjust?
- How will we handle not knowing a single person in our new community?
- Will I be working considerably more and not see my family?
- How will I handle the logistics of the move from here to there?
- Will I rent an apartment or buy a home and how will I find one?

As you can see there are an infinite number of questions and potential problems that come with a new job in a new state and, realistically, there are absolutely no answers to the above question until you cut all connections to your old job and start the new one which is filled with considerable anxiety and uncertainty.

With stock market investing you have the following questions. The risks with stock market investing may seem daunting today but your job is to minimize these risks by acquiring knowledge, by constantly learning, by repeating your review of the charts until you can see them in your sleep.

STOCK MARKET RISKS:

- What should I buy? (answer: TQQQ)
- When should I buy? (answer: when your indicators tell you)
- When should I sell? (answer: when your indicators tell you)
- How much should I buy? (answer: when ready, your investment balance – remember "Compound Investing")
- How do I know the exact day to buy? (answer: when your indicators tell you)
- How do I know the exact day to sell? (answer: when your indicators tell you)

Each of these questions already has an answer unlike the new job list that has no answers. So you tell me which one of the above scenarios has higher risk?

You are not entering into any trade blindly since we have covered every one of the above points in great detail. I have tried to cover every scenario you may encounter when reviewing your charts. By you reviewing every potential buy and sell point over a ten year period there are not many scenarios left that you haven't already reviewed. Again, before committing a single dollar to a new trade, you must review, review, and review again. By entering into paper trades for a few weeks or months or until you feel comfortable committing real money to the transaction you should be on the sidelines watching and learning. To this day I continue to compare today's charts to previous ones over the years to see if I see a similar setup as in the past. I always find numerous examples to compare to today.

I will admit that it is easier to see the next trade setting up in hindsight when backdating but stack the deck in your favor by clicking from one day to the next on your historic charts, adding a buy line to the chart then advancing to the next day to see the outcome of your decision. This is the only way to backdate your buy/sell choices. If you take a shortcut and don't do the above, you are taking a shortcut on your study time. The more time you put into studying the charts the more confident you will be when it is time to actually buy with real money. One downside of trading with paper money is that you don't have any real skin in the game. There is an artificial feeling of satisfaction since no adrenaline is pumped into your system. When you start to trade with real money you will be feeling unsure and attempt to second guess yourself. This is normal so until you generate confidence with a few early successful buy/sell transactions you will feel shaky.

You may read that you shouldn't commit more than 2% of your excess capital on any one trade known as position sizing, or that you should always have a 2%, 5%, or 10% stop-loss with each trade or that you shouldn't hold more than four positions at any one time. These are valid point when investing in common stock or other types of more volatile investments and, also, if you do not know what you are doing.

I feel common technology stocks such as Facebook, Twitter, etc. are considerably riskier than investing in an ETF like TQQQ which tracks the overall technology sector like the NASDAQ 100. As we have reviewed earlier, the NASDAQ 100 is the market average made up of 100 technology stocks so you are not dealing with only one stock. Also buying more than one stock on the NASDAQ list increases the risk for a price surprise and that you will divert your focus by attempting to anticipate each day's price change for multiple investments. Your job is to simplify not complicate. The least number of diversions the better. That is why I stick to only four indicators out of hundreds. That is why I stick to only one investment, TQQQ, since I know this ETF intimately and can almost anticipate when it will be moving up and down. With practice you can do the same.

When reading about stock information on the Internet, I have found that the suggestions as to when to buy and when to sell are so general as to be worthless. Also, I have purposely avoided talking about stock chart patterns such as pennants, cup and handle, ascending triangles, falling wedges, etc. These patterns are subjective and left to the interpretation of the individual observer. They are almost like naming constellations in the night sky, one may see the star pattern and another may not. I have covered only the ones that are most important since they come up all the time:

- Double and triple tops and bottoms
- Trendlines and channels for uptrends and downtrends

TRADING DIARY

A trading diary is just that. It documents each buy/sell transaction to review at a later date. The Figure 1a-c in the Introduction is a trading diary. It documents your success or failure over time and allows you to see how your initial dollar investment has grown. I encourage you to keep a similar diary for your back dating research and your paper trades as well since this is your practice time. You want to get the feel of all the details of each transaction to be able to review them later if your results were not what you expected. Even though you are initially trading with paper money there is a natural tendency to "feel like you are missing out" by passing on upcoming setups in real-time. Be aware of this emotion and let it go. There will be numerous more setups in the near future. On your trading diary you can even add a section for each indicator before your buy day to document if it is flashing a green or red signal which is what I did initially. This way all the items involved in your decision are documented. You can review later to see if you followed all the success factors or skipped a few which resulted in less than the maximum profit per trade.

These steps are very important since you are developing working habits for success which you will use again and again with each trade. All the indicators have to be aligned each time for each buy and sell for the trade to work. If your buy point is perfect but the sell point is missed, your profit could vanish. Looking back over your trading diary while reviewing the chart of that transaction in hindsight will give you the clues what you either missed or disregarded to cause the loss. Next time you will do better if you are diligent in following all the steps prior to buying and selling. Remember, to maximize your profit for each trade, there is one best buy day and price and one best sell day and price. I am not saying that you have to hit perfection each and every time. What I am saying is that you want to aim for perfection and achieve excellence. Even if you miss by a few percentage points per trade in your first few trades the overall result will still be significantly positive. But you do want to continue to improve. On your charts you can use a green and red vertical line for the ideal buy and sell day and price and then two different color lines for your actual buy and sell day and price. Over time your custom colors will no longer be used and your green and red line will be the actual price that you bought and sold.

One last point. I have modified "The Plan" that I discussed in Chapter Three which is a step-by-step checklist to get started and added step #4 below:

THE PLAN

1. Open a brokerage account with one of the above investment companies (not a mutual fund company like Fidelity Investments or Vanguard).

2. Once opened link your checking or savings account to this brokerage account (if you need help call the investment company).

3. Transfer money into this new brokerage account in any amount that you wish (I funded my account with $3,000).

4. Open a Roth IRA with the investment company and move the $3,000 to the Roth IRA (I will explain the pros and cons of this step below).

5. Research your chart data as outlined above.

6. After you feel confidant and based on the information in Chapter Four start buying and selling TQQQ.

ROTH IRA

Now, what is this about a Roth IRA in Step 4 of The Plan? Assume you are in the 22% tax bracket so capital gains (the profit on your buy/sell transactions) are taxable at the end of the year. Once this tax is subtracted from your profit, the balance to invest at the next buy signal is 22% less. If this process is multiplied by the number of buy/sell transactions from 2010 thru 2020 you would have a considerably smaller balance to trade with.

Here are some advantages of a Roth IRA:

1. There is no tax to be paid at the end of each year like on your cash account.

2. There is no tax on any cash withdrawals. Since you are adding after-tax money to fund the Roth IRA. Any withdrawals of profit from this account are tax free.

3. You have to keep all the money in the account for 5 years from inception if the profit is from investment income (which it is). This is a good thing since it forces you to be disciplined to NOT take out profits therefore reducing the cash on your next buy transaction (remember "Compound Investing").

4. There are valid tax reasons to withdraw money from the account before 59 1/2 like education expenses, first-time home purchase, uninsured medical expenses, but not just to spend on stuff.

5. On the downside, the tax free proceeds can't be withdrawn for any other reason than those in step 4 until age 59 ½. On the upside, this could be your retirement tax free income unlike a traditional IRA which taxes cash withdrawals after retirement.

Consult a tax professional about comparing the Roth IRA, traditional IRA, and a cash trading account before proceeding. Take a closer look at all the pros and cons of this account but the main pro is that all your money stays in the account tax-free to really pump up your year to year profits. Once your eligible to withdraw the money all the proceeds are tax free and you will be a millionaire!

SUMMARY POINTS:

- **Only start your investment account with a modest amount of money you can afford to do without or that is not needed to pay bills or for emergencies. You may have initial losses until you get comfortable making your buy/sell decisions at the correct day so don't get discouraged. There will be plenty of other opportunities to make money.**

- If you don't have the initial cash balance to start trading and need to save this money, view this time period as your learning phase. Take advantage of this time to study, study, study.

- If viewed analytically, stock market investing is a smaller risk than taking a jet on a vacation or moving to a new state for a new job. For your vacation you have to plan every detail so nothing goes wrong so you are minimizing your risk. You will take the same steps to minimize risk with stock market investing, reviewing each step so nothing goes wrong from the safety of your computer.

- Make sure all your indicators are positioned properly before making the buy or sell decision.

- Use a trading diary to document your paper trades before starting real money trades.

- And most important, stick to The Plan.

CHAPTER EIGHT

Summary of All Points

So, here we are near the end of the book. Hopefully, you have been filled with many new idea on how to make big money in the stock market using trend trades. I have tried to impart my experience making these trades day-in and day-out. Since I'm a regular guy and have been able to do it you certainly can do it too. I have also given you a great deal of detail so you are covered against almost every eventually which I feel is lacking in many of the competing eBooks on the Internet and in hard-copy on this topic. Believe me that I have read most of them. I have also tried to give you these details from the perspectives of a non-professional investor just like myself. I have developed a relatively simple system that works consistently. I suggest that you review this quick section and then go over each section of the book, especially the graphs, since they are the actual buy and sell trades. Go slow, reread each section of each chapter as many time as needed. Match the graphs in the book to the actual graphs online so you see that I have given you real information from actual charts. Go back to 2010 and work your way to the present while looking at the graphs enclosed. This is the only way you can identify my charts with your charts. See if you would have made the same buy and sell decisions as I have. Here is a quick synopsis of each chapter.

Chapter One Summary Points – What is Trend Trading:

- Day trading is holding a security for one day with potentially many trades in that one day. By the end of the day you don't hold any positions.

- Trend trading is holding a security for days, weeks, or months depending on the length of the trend. Sometimes the trend is long and will last from one to many months while you are watching the price each day as it continues the trend upwards to make sure the price stays on track. Sometimes the trend is very short being one or more weeks. During this short trend you have to be vigilant each day for the reversal which will come. Practice getting your eye used to how the trends work by reviewing past trends that were long and short. Generally, after one or two long trends lasting months, the price will start to get choppy as the opposite action of the last few months. If the price is moving sideways, you can make money with short trends. If the price starts to drop it could drop significantly. During this time it is best to sit on the sidelines and listen to the commentators issue doom and gloom forecasts that this time is the end of the stock market as we know it. Looking over many years of past ups and downs you will know better and the good times will eventually return just as the rain is followed by the sun and the night is followed by the day repeated endlessly again and again.

- Focus on the price oscillation of your security to determine your buy and sell point. The price will oscillate up and down repeatedly over many days with many days between trades while you are waiting for the next buy point to occur. This oscillation is the heart of trend trading with the price rising, reaching a zenith, then dropping just to be repeated again.

- You have plenty of time to find the right buy and sell point when trend trading. Remember, there is an exact day to buy and sell but you can be late by one or two days as long as you make money. As you get more experienced, your buy and sell days will occur closer and closer to the actual "best" day to buy and sell.

Chapter Two Summary Points – Trading Platforms:

- You will use a trading platform to buy and sell your securities. Pick one that has the features you want then set up your account. Link your checking or savings account to your new trading account and transfer in money. Most of the investment companies now offer commission-free trades which is to your advantage. Take a look at all the large companies to see which fit is the best for you. Most of them are similar to each other so pick the one that has the most services that you will take advantage of. Don't worry about esoteric services you would never use such as option trading. This type of trading is significantly more complicated than the system I have outlined in this book. Recently, Ameritrade and Charles Schwab have merged creating one mega investment company with no trading costs which is to your advantage.

- The price chart has basic components or indicators that will not change once they are set up the way you want. Pick a charting program that is easy to use, easy to look at, easy to set up, and available on all platforms. At home, I use TradingView on my PC and iPad, at work I use it on my PC with each instance in a standard browser like Chrome, IOS, and Edge. When I change the view even slightly that view is saved online and when I move from work to home, that same view is updated on my home PC automatically. This is pretty cool so I'm talking about real convenience. I used to use thinkorswim by Ameritrade but the platform has to be downloaded to each device separately and can only be viewed on that individual computer or device you are using at that time. There is a separate download for each PC, iPad, iPhone, and Android with no auto updating of custom drawings, etc., unless you are using the same device. Therefore, for each device you would have to configure all the indicators to mirror each other which can be a chore. I use TD Ameritrade Mobile on my Android phone and iPad only to make trades and not to view the charts.

- Focus on the price oscillation of your security to determine your buy and sell point. As I have explained with numerous charts, the price in relation to the four indicators is your signal to buy or sell. As the price is dropping at some point it will level out even for a few days. That is when the indicators flash the correct buy point all in unison. Remember, all the indicators have to be giving you the same message on the 1-day chart and there should be corroboration on the 2-day chart of some of the indicators especially the moving average. Practice spending only 10 minutes per day when you are fully up to speed with your trades.

- Use sell stops as an insurance policy when you are away from your computer for an extended time. Generally, you would set a sell stop in your trading software a few percentage points below the current price. As the price increases you can update your sell stop to go up proportionally. If you will be away from your computer for some days or some weeks you can set the sell stop once and forget about it. If you are able to, you still may want to check in on the price in your browser periodically to make sure everything is on track. Once you are familiar with what to look for, it is easy to spot a change in direction and identify the sell day.

Chapter Three Summary Points – What to Buy:

- Rather than buying individual stocks buy an ETF and, specifically, TQQQ. Common stocks are prone to significant reversals with no notice and for no apparent reason. Even when earnings and sales are stronger than last quarter, the stock price can drop for no reason that is apparent to a lay person. For example, if sales and earnings are strong but guidance (future earnings and/or sales) is expected to be slightly lower, the stock price will tank. Remember, the stock market is unforgiving with a herd mentality so when one runs for the hills they all do and you are left holding a stock at a lower price which is the opposite of your goal. Stock prices based on the above are very vulnerable every quarter when companies announce their earnings which is four times a year so that the price can go up or down suddenly. ETFs on the other hand don't have quarterly earnings announcements so you have just removed a very large uncertainty from your trading.

- The NASDAQ 100 market average, represented by the ETF QQQ is a 1:1 match with the NASDAQ as far as the chart is concerned so when the NASDAQ 100 goes up 1% the QQQ goes up 1% also. What I have recommended is the TQQQ which is leveraged 3:1 so when the NASDAQ 100 goes up 1%, TQQQ goes up 3%. The only time this is a problem is if you are not watching your 1-day/2-day chart. This is like being behind the wheel of your car and texting at the same time – you are not watching the road. Obviously, something bad is going to happen so don't be surprised when it does. If you are not watching your charts daily but only once in a while and no more, your eyes are off the road. While your back is turned the price will drop. This can happen with any stock, any ETF, or any other type of investment. Appreciation requires attention to detail so you must treat it seriously.

- Get a graphing program like thinkorswim or TradingView. This is required for your success. Don't rely on anyone else to tell you when to buy or sell. That is giving up your responsibility for your own money. You must be responsible for this yourself. I like TradingView since it will show the same view on any device that has a browser. You don't have to adjust indicators based on the device you are using.

- Keep reading and studying – never stop. The only way you will be successful is if you continue to learn. Don't make this book the last one you read on investing. Remember, if all or most of my ideas resonate with you and you want to emulate my plan, don't stray too far from the core principals as outlined here. Think and plan before changing ideas too quickly or radically except if you don't agree with the ideas expressed here at all. If my plan makes no sense to you or appears too radical for your taste please ignore any and all of my information. If, on the other hand, you find the ideas listed here to your liking, then go for it.

- Don't forget to practice on paper trades to get a feel for the price movement on the graph over various timeframes. Don't rush this part of it. Take all the time you need. You may get overconfident and start trading sooner than you are ready. You will only lose money so slow down.

- Follow "The Plan". If you feel that the Roth IRA is not for you, that is fine. It is just my idea to 1) maximize profits, have a forced savings account with which to retire a millionaire, and 3) have a deterrent to spending the money before you balance has increase to make a significant difference via "Compound Investing". You will feel the excitement that everything is working as it should as your percentage profits and cash accumulate. This is not a get rich quick scheme. It will take time, focus, and dedication to stay the course. You will also want to keep your gains intact for the inevitable loss. If you have a few wins then spend your gains you will have that much less to invest to keep the momentum going.

Chapter Four Summary Points – Indicators:

- Indicators coinciding with price provide buy and sell points. Remember, all or most of the indicators should match the price movement. They are there simply for corroboration of where the price is going. All of them work on momentum. As the momentum of the price increases, the indicators shoot up strongly. As the price momentum slows down the indicators begin to flatten out. One point to watch for here is that the indicators may start to flatten as the momentum of the price begins to slow even while the price continues to rise but at a slower pace. This is why you have other indicators as well as the 2-day chart to refer to. You want to stay in the trade as long as both charts and all indicators are showing the same view. You may get one indicator that turns negative while all the rest are still climbing so hold on a little longer. If they most or all turn negative then it is time to sell.

- Consider the four indicators that work for me as your starting point. Start by sticking to these indicators:

  - Hull Moving Average (HMA set to 20)

  - MACD (set to 9,10,9)

  - Stochastic Momentum (set to 14, 3, 5)

  - CCI (set to 15)

- If you want to experiment with other indicators there are hundreds to choose from but keep the above four always available to go back to and record the settings so you don't forget them. The price movement coincides with the indicator movement to give you a 3-D view of where the price is going. It can go only in three directions, up, sideways, or down which is reinforced with the movement of the indicators.

- Keep it simple and don't choose too many indicators as they will just confuse you. Remember, the simpler the better. The more indicators you choose the more confusing your charts will get. In the past I have had as many as 12 indicators and I have learned that more is definitely not better. In fact, the opposite is true, the more you choose the more confusing your screen will get. Some will contradict others adding to more confusion which will cause you to lose money. Remember, simple is good and the less you have to distract or confuse you the better.

- Indicators work during upturns and downturns. Even during a larger downturn there are still many opportunities to make money with smaller upturns within the larger downturn. Just watch the indicators for buying opportunities. Choosing a longer time frame on your chart may cause you to stay with a trade even as the price on the 1-day chart starts dropping. If the 1-day chart says sell, the longer timeframe chart may continue to stay positive. See Figure 97 below. The 1-day chart has just flashed a sell signal as shown by the price moving below the moving average with all three other indicators moving in a negative direction then rebounding, yet, the 2-day upward move is still intact with no real negatives.

- Indicators coinciding with price provide buy and sell points. Use only these four indicators: Hull Moving Average, MACD, Stochastic Momentum, and CCI or Commodity Channel Index.

- Indicators help visualize the price movement oscillation more completely showing overbought and oversold areas. Traditionally overbought areas are areas where the price has not stayed for very long so it is considered an extreme before it started to move down. The same is true of oversold areas. These areas represent extremely low price areas where the price has lingered for a relatively short time before moving up again. Remember, the indicator can in high or low areas for some time as the price is still rising or going lower so pay attention.

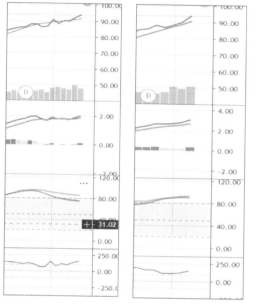

Figure 97: 12/23/19 – 1/09/20: 1-day chart showing some weakness but 2-day chart still showing strength

- Prices will move up significantly and then down suddenly so the indicators help keep you on course. It takes about 25% of the time for the price to drop as it took to go up the same dollar amount so anticipate sudden price drops and slower price increases.

Chapter Five Summary Points – Timeframes:

- Timeframes can be long or short. Very short intraday timeframes are for day traders and very long ones are for buy-and-hold investors. A one week timeframe will get you in and out of a trade too late resulting in reduced profits. Use the 1-day and 2-day chart timeframes to view price movement that is most accurate for 4-5 trades per year where you will capture virtually all upward moves.

- Consolidation periods occur when the price has just concluded an up or down move and is now moving sideways before the next leg up or down.

- Step patterns occur when the price moves up or down in a step-wise pattern indicating a pause in the movement before the next move up or down.

- Be on the lookout for double and triple tops and bottoms as they preview the next move up or down.

- Support and resistance lines are your visual cue that the price may not go lower during support and may not go higher during resistance.

- Trendlines and channels visually show continuing movement up or down until the price breaks above or below the channel lines signaling a change in direction.

Chapter Six Summary Points – Mind Over Matter:

- Emotion most definitely enters into your buy/sell decisions. The psychology of the market can influence your decisions from day to day. Avoid reading inflammatory headlines in online investment websites since they will influence you to buy and sell at the wrong time. If you look back at past price moves on your charts, you will have no memory of what was occurring in the news, the economy, world events, etc. to cause the price to move up or down at that moment in time. At the time I'm sure there were valid reasons why the price was moving up or down but those reasons are lost from memory. These current events should have no influence on your buy/sell decisions and the price and indicator movement should be the only factors influencing you from day to day.

- Look at the longer 2-day timeframe chart to corroborate what the shorter 1-day timeframe chart is flashing. Stay with the trade until almost all indicators in both timeframes show weakness or you may kick yourself out of the trade too early. When this occurs, and it will occur more frequently at the beginning of your investment journey, analyze where the price is along its path upward. If you feel that the price is past the midway point resist the urge to jump in only to have the price drop on that same day or the next few days. Remember that the price will drop faster and more powerfully than it took to move up.

- You will have many more opportunities in the coming days, months, and years to make plenty of profits so don't get greedy and want every move to be a winner. Don't forget that you are learning so learn from your past mistakes. Try to stay emotionally neutral. Tap into yourself to see if you feel like you are missing the golden opportunity of a lifetime to make money on this particular day. This is a sure sign that emotion is in control of your decision. Try this exercise to know what I mean. Purposely avoid entering into the next trade in spite of what the headlines are screaming or what your feelings are telling you. Watch dispassionately as the price proceeds upward. Resist the urge to jump in. Be aware of the "feeling of missing out". Watch as the price reaches its top and corrects downward while always watching your indicators, then consider entering the trade on the next move up. This exercise will teach you what the unemotional feeling is like by only watching the price and indicators. With your next trade remind yourself what the feeling is like to make the trade, watch the price rise, reach the top and start to descend down without any excitement or fear. This is the state of consciousness you need to be in for each trade to succeed. This feeling will make you big money.

Chapter Seven Summary Points – Money Management and Risk:

- Only start your investment account with a modest amount of money you can afford to do without to pay bills or for emergencies. You may have some initial small losses until you get comfortable making your buy/sell decisions on the correct day so don't get discouraged. There will be plenty of other opportunities to make money. Remember, the train goes from station to station so if you miss this train another one will follow shortly.

- If viewed analytically, stock market investing is a smaller risk than taking a jet on a vacation or moving to another state for a new job. For your vacation you have to plan every detail so nothing goes wrong so you are minimizing your risk. You will take the same steps to minimize risk with stock market investing, reviewing each step so that nothing goes wrong.

CHAPTER NINE

Questions and Answers

I was planning of ending the book here but a colleague of mine suggested adding a question and answer chapter to answer some common questions that you and many like you may have asked so here we go. I thought this was a good idea since it allows you to read answers to common questions that were not covered elsewhere in the book. It will also act as a further review besides the above chapter review.

- **Question**: How do I get started in the stock market?

- **Answer**: From Chapter One in this book to the last chapter, you must read and study then read the book again. As in any new endeavor, repetition and practice are required until that new skill is mastered. This takes time since we learn at one rate. Throw in the demands of family and job and we have even less time to study a new skill we are totally unfamiliar with. To complicate this process, there are thousands of ideas on the Internet and in books which adds to the dizzying complexity of an activity that can be quite simple once mastered. I have narrowed this universe of differing ideas to just a few simple principles. If you start with the first and work your way to the last, the end will not feel so impossible to reach. The first step is to want to make this change from ignorance to informed, then to want to make money simply and easily by spending the least amount of time managing this new activity. Only then will your mind be ready to want to learn stock market investing in a way that makes sense and can be duplicated again and again with astounding results.

- **Question**: What type of investment should I start with?

- **Answer**: I wanted to start with the simplest investment in a field of 3,000 companies represented in the stock market alone. I narrowed this number to just the three most common market averages, the Dow, the S&P, and the NASDAQ 100 since almost all investment companies try to match the performance of these averages with individual stocks and fail. I then chose the NASDAQ since it represented the highest performing technology companies. I then chose a surrogate for this market average, the ETF QQQ which is a 1:1 percent appreciation comparison. I then wanted the highest percent appreciation possible so switched to the TQQQ which provides a 3:1 return so I broke the whole complex process down to a few simple steps.

- **Question**: Suppose I am less risk averse, what should I do?

- **Answer**: In my system, you could choose to follow the QQQ at 1:1 or TQQQ at 3:1 using the 1-day/2-day charts, 1-week/2-week charts or longer. The choice is yours. This would provide a wider field of view as an advantage but with a disadvantage that these charts are slower so would get you into and out of the trade later. The main idea is to make significantly more money than a money market account and be able to sleep at night. I would suggest starting your training experience with the 1-day/2-day charts to see how comfortable you are with this view. As I had done in the past, I tried different time frames while going reviewing prior dates, or back testing, to see how fast or slow these charts were while fitting this into my risk level. I finally settled on the 1-day/2-day as my final time frames as the combination that worked for me the best. With my increased risk tolerance I then switched from QQQ to TQQQ and then added SQQQ.

- **Question:** Isn't is safer to be more diversified?

- **Answer:** Common knowledge says yes but l have found that diversification adds to the stock market complexity which causes confusion and lower profits. This is the opposite of what we are trying to achieve. Therefore, less diversification creates simplicity and less confusion and higher profits. Diversification is necessary when we do not know what we are doing so we are spreading the risk of ignorance over a wider area. We cannot create more confidence from less knowledge. Remember that "market gurus" assume we are not at all familiar with the working of the stock market so diversification among many stocks or investments like an 80% stock/20% bond allocation is more prudent. I say, nonsense, since by this time in your learning you are more knowledgeable and confident than 95% of average investors. This is a tremendous advantage to making big money in the stock market by trend trading.

- **Question:** Should I have a cash account or another type of account that I trade in?

- **Answer:** Trading in and out of a cash account makes good sense if you are not familiar with a standard IRA or Roth IRA. I have suggested a Roth IRA for a few reasons. First, your appreciation is tax free since you are investing with money that you have already paid tax on. Second, your gains are locked in for five years so the natural tendency to spend these gains whenever you may want to buy stuff is eliminated so is a forced savings. Third, using "Compound Investing" your profits are multiplied many time over in a way that cannot be achieved using any other type of account. With a traditional IRA, you will have to pay taxes on any distributions after retirement unlike the Roth IRA where distributions are tax free at 59 1/2 . Talk to a tax professional about the pros and cons before moving forward.

- **Question:** If I follow your plan how often should I check charts and enjoy the appreciation?

- **Answer:** Once you have chosen to follow my plan, you must get into the habit of checking your charts no more than ten minutes each day. Any more and you will start second guessing your buy/sell decisions which will lead to losses and failure. As to your appreciation, I recommend adding only the percent gain of each trade into your trading journal with buy and sell prices but with no ending balance. This process focuses your mind to separate one trade from the next and keeps your mind only focused on the buy and sell point. Your goal is to have a positive percent gain with each trade however small or large and stay in the present. When looking at a cash balance increasing, human nature will start getting you nervous about that balance dropping and your focus will be on the balance and not on the currant trade.

- **Question:** Should I keep abreast of the daily investment news?

- **Answer:** Definitely not. The daily business news is inflammatory and will just cause you to get emotional leading to fear about the stock market and daily events which influence the market. This is the opposite of your goal. Your goal is to be emotionally separated from your trades and to make your buy/sell decisions unemotionally. Emotionality leads to mistakes which lead to financial losses.

- **Question:** What should I do if I only have a small amount of money to invest?

- **Answer:** You can invest any amount that you are comfortable with. Starting small prepares you to stay emotionally stable and as your profit percentages increase while using "Compound Investing", your confidence will build. If you are comfortable starting with more, all the better. You may want to take part of your yearly tax refund and add to your investment. This amount of money will go much further to add to your riches than buying stuff.

- **Question:** What percentage return should I aim for?

- **Answer:** The average rate of return of the S&P from 1957 onward has been +8% per year. In good times, technology stocks like Apple, Microsoft, and others my provide a return of about +20-30% per year. Using my system your rate of return should average over +100% per year. This sounds impossible but reading this book will show you how to achieve this tremendous rate of appreciation step by step. On average, your goal will be a +25% return on each trade with some trades in the single digits and some in the triple digits with most in the high double digits.

- **Question:** Isn't investing in TQQQ very risky?

- **Answer:** TQQQ at a 3:1 return is no riskier than buying and selling QQQ at a 1:1 return which is a direct surrogate of the NASDAQ 100 index. The charts comparing the two support this view. In my opinion, this ETF is considerably less risky than buying individual stocks with their unknowns like quarterly earnings announcements and unwise business decisions executives make all the time. Additionally, your performance will totally depend on the stocks you pick with some trending up while some begin to trend down. By using this strategy you are diluting your capital to those stocks that start to move sideways for extended periods or start moving down. This is counterproductive to achieving the highest return with the least risk. The more investments in your portfolio the greater the risk that your returns will be diminished. Remember, we want simple.

- **Question:** Should I use dollar cost averaging to make my investment?

- **Answer:** Dollar cost averaging means that you are investing the same dollar amount on a fixed schedule so when the stock price is higher you are buying fewer shares at a higher price and when the price is lower, you are buying a greater number of shares at a lower price so that the investment cost is averaged. This process is the opposite of what my system advocates since it assumes that you do not know how to invest any other way. In my system, you start with a fixed amount of money. As the price of TQQQ appreciates you are selling at a higher price on the correct day which you will see coming in advance as your indicators tell you. At the next upturn you will then buy a greater number of shares with the entire higher balance in your account and make the next trade. This is called "Compound Investing" and is at the heart of the fabulous appreciation that you cannot achieve any other way.

- **Question**: Should I be paying attention to the financials of a company I want to invest in?

- **Answer**: My system is based on technical analysis to tell you when to buy and sell so you are only focused on what information your charts and indicators are telling you. Your question pertains to fundamental analysis which is the study of a company's financial strength or weakness. My system is focused on simplicity while fundamental analysis should be left to the accountants since it is very much more complicated.

- **Question**: Why do market crashes happen?

- **Answer**: Markets have an upward bias so all the private individuals and companies that buy stocks and other investment vehicles want to make money by having the markets constantly going up. Just like any other type of increase in nature, prices need to find an equilibrium between very high and very low. Human nature, on the other hand, energized by excitement and fear wants to make money endlessly so, in effect, we are out of sync with nature. The laws of economics act as a brake from our human tendencies getting out of control but our human nature fights against this counterbalance so at some point, prices are either considered overbought or oversold. A climax top is the visual representation of our excitement to want the uptrend of prices to go on indefinitely. Normally, at this point it takes one incident however minor for reason to prevail which triggers prices to come crashing down to more moderate levels and the process is repeated. Simply put, this up and down process is just watching human nature at work.

- **Question**: How much does program trading contribute to prices rising irrationally and then crashing?

- **Answer**: Program trading refers to computer algorithms that automatically buy and sell stocks at a very high rate of speed but faster than a human could do the same task. These thousands of buy/sell orders are executed in milliseconds to make as high a profit as possible in the shortest amount of time when prices are rising as well as when they are falling. This process accounts for 50-60% of all trades on the exchanges. Program trading definitely contributes to dramatic ups and precipitous downs in the market averages especially during large news events when there is indecision in the markets. At the same time this indecision leads to market turmoil in other countries as well and fear becomes the global emotion. Following my system, you will be out of the trade before a market crash occurs. As I have shown you with multiple examples, it is not hard to see a major market crash coming. You will then be watching dispassionately as 1) the markets go significantly lower while you are on the sidelines or, 2) you have purchased SQQQ and your profits skyrocket. During the market crash of

2020 I switched to SQQQ on 2/212/20 at $17.39 and dispassionately watched the price go to $32.27 for a profit of +86%.

- **Question**: If there is a crash and I am not out of the market, should I sell?

- **Answer**: Following the system I have explained you will be able to make the decision to know when to buy, when to sell, and when to hold in advance of any significant market downturn. As a result, in every past crash you would have been safely out of the market at the correct time ahead of the first day of the crash. There would be no guessing but a clear, unemotional decision to buy, hold, or sell. If you were watching a climax top approaching you would have known to sell a week or more in advance. That is the beauty or my system. It will always warn you of impending disaster which could be a drop of a few percent or a more dramatic downturn.

- **Question**: What happens if I can't duplicate your performance in Figure 1a-c?

- **Answer**: I do not expect you to come close to this performance at your stage of learning. Since you bought this book I do expect you to read, learn, study the charts from ten years ago diligently, and practice many times before you are even ready to trade with real dollars. You will be doing all these preliminary steps and trading on paper. Only when you feel more confident to try the principles explained here will you put your toe in the water and try your first small money trade. At this point I expect you to still be very nervous and watch your charts constantly. Now I would recommend that you practice non emotional behavior by gradually stop watching the charts every five minutes. Practice checking into your charts only once a day and then for ten minutes then move your attention to other things. By practicing in this way will you be ready to commit more money to your next trade. Eventually, you will be entering trade after trade with your entire balance and achieving tremendous financial success with each trade.

- **Question**: After I have invested in TQQQ and the price is going up as expected, can I then also invest in a hot technology stock like Amazon, Apple, or Microsoft also?

- **Answer**: You certainly can do this if you wish. My recommendation is to stay away from multiple other individual stocks in any category and stick to TQQQ. The reason for this is simple. The more stocks you invest in, in addition to TQQQ, the more complicated your focus will be with these other investments. I recommend that you stay 100% focused on TQQQ only and no other stock since other stocks will not behave exactly like TQQQ since this ETF represents the whole NASDAQ 100 universe. In the universe, some stocks are going up while others are going down. You are making a bet that the stocks you choose will go up like TQQQ. In the comparison charts in prior pages I showed how these "hot" stocks did not come close to the appreciation of TQQQ. The reason for this is that these stocks are contributing to the overall price of the NASDAQ 100 at a 1:1 ratio while TQQQ is creating results at a 3:1 ratio so these individual stock could never triple their appreciation like TQQQ can.

- **Question**: I am watching the market crash in 2020 and prices dropping precipitously. When will the momentum stop and prices start rising?

- **Answer**: Your charts and indicators will answer this question for you. They will tell you when the momentum is slowing down since your indicators measure momentum directly. Your 1-day price graph and moving average will show your entry price which will be corroborated by looking at your 2-day graph. In addition, using trend lines and/or price channels will tell you when to avoid false temporary up moves. Looking back over each market crash I have reviewed will instruct you when to enter the market again. This is not guess work but facts based on numerous past market crashes.

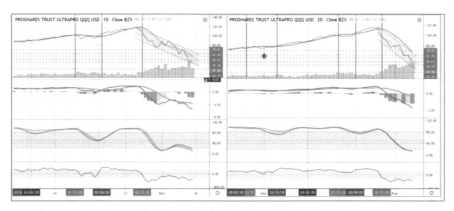

Figure 98: 2/21/20 – 3/13/20: 1-day/2-day chart showing TQQQ

Figure 98 illustrates my point. We were out of the trade on 2/21/20 and watched the 1-day chart in fascination as the price of TQQQ dropped from a high of $118.06 to the current price of $47.57 or -60% with the corresponding uptrend of SQQQ (Figure 99). See the channel I have drawn to show the path of the price as it works its way down. The red dotted horizontal lines mark past support and resistance zones where the price will either pause and reverse or break through to continue the trend down which it has done through four support price lines already. Now, looking at the 2-day chart we do not see any sign of an impending reversal either with the price or with any of the indicators. Just as a reminder, the price on both charts always drops in a zig zag pattern and never goes down in a straight line. We are looking for the price to flatten out and break above the top downward line of the channel on the 1-day chart and, also, break above the moving average on the 2-day chart. As of 3/12/2020 there is no indication that this downward trend will be reversing any time soon.

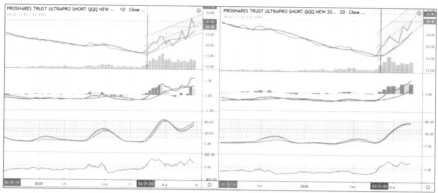

Figure 99: 2/21/20 – 3/12/20: 1-day/2-day chart showing SQQQ

- **Question:** How do I emotionally handle a final balance of $300,000 starting from my $3,000 initial investment?

- **Answer:** I would say "Happily". Revel in your achievement but stay focused on the next trade and its double digit percent increase. Do not get enthralled with the dollar balance as this will cause you to make mistakes on your net trade. I would recommend hiding the balance column in your electronic trading diary so you do not see this day in and day out. This will force your eyes to only focus on the entry and exit day of each trade. Viewing the percent appreciation is good to encourage you with positive achievement. With the next trade, look for an average appreciation of +25% or $75,000 so, if your peek, your balance will now be $375,000 by using "Compound Investing".

- **Question:** How did you create this system?

- **Answer:** I started with a process first expounded by Aristotle 2,000 years ago called "First Principles" which is a way to simplify complex problems into smaller steps. The first step is to identify a problem and its common assumptions:

  - **Problem:** The stock market is too complex to understand.

  - **Assumption:** *It is complex so I cannot make money easily.* This way of thinking stops our forward movement before it eve starts since it is the thinking of most people who do not have knowledge of or experience with the stock market

The second step is to break down the problem into its basic truths:

- **Truth #1:** *There are many ways to analyze stock market information.*

- **Solution:** I must, therefore, narrow down the analysis of the stock market to technical analysis vs fundamental analysis.

- **Truth #2:** *It is complex because there are too many stocks to choose from.*

- **Solution:** I must, therefore, narrow the universe of stocks down to only one (TQQQ).

- **Truth #3:** *There are over 300 different indicators to choose from.*

- **Solution:** I must, therefore, narrow the universe of indicators down to only four.

- **Truth #4:** *There are many different time frames to view TQQQ.*

- **Solution:** I must, therefore, narrow the universe of time frames to only two, 1-day and 2-day charts.

In this way a complex problem like making big money in the stock market by trend trading becomes just a number of manageable steps to our ultimate goal.

You can read about Aristotle's First Principles at this link: (*https://medium.com/the-mission/elon-musks-3-step-first-principles-thinking-how-to-think-and-solve-difficult-problems-like-a-ba1e73a9f6c0*), accessed March 13, 2020.

- **Question:** What are some general rules that apply to the stock market that match those in this book?

- **Answer:** General stock market rules include those developed by famed investor Bob Farrell many years ago that still apply today and are expanded upon in this book:

- o *"**Markets tend to return to the mean over time**"*: Long stretches of an up market are balanced with similar stretches of a down market.

- o *"**Excesses in one direction will lead to an opposite excess in the other direction**":* As in the above bullet point but could be applied to a small time frame as well.

- o *"**There are no new eras – excesses are never permanent**"*: Hot stocks during the dot.com era fade and a new group always takes their place.

- o *"**Exponential rapidly rising or falling markets usually go further than you think, but they do not correct by going sideways**"*: A strong trend can last a long time but the correction will be strong and swift in the opposite direction as during a market crash in 25% of the time as it took to go up.

- o *"**The public buys the most at the top and the least at the bottom**"*: Average "investors" do not know when a climax top is imminent and buy more near that top. The reverse is true during severe market corrections in that these same "investors" will wait too long as the market corrects then will sell at the bottom since they think the down trend has more to go. At this point in your reading you know better and will be out at the top and will reenter at the bottom.

- o *"**Fear and greed are stronger than long-term resolve**":* To make big money in the stock market using swing trades you need to be making these trades without emotion. These emotions will lose you money every time.

- o *"**Markets are strongest when they are broad and weakest when they are narrow to a handful of blue-chip names**"*: A broad market move up includes all markets, Dow, NASDAQ, and S&P and will be stronger than one which only includes one of these groups and not all.

- o *"**Bear markets have three stages – sharp down, reflexive rebound and a drawn-out fundamental downtrend**":* As I am writing this, the markets have all incurred a significant drop that have not yet included a reflex rebound, but they will drop lower in these three moves down.

- o **"When all the experts and forecasts agree – something else is going on":** Too much enthusiastically positive consensus will lead to the opposite action or a market drop and vice versa.

- ○ **"Bull markets are more fun than bear markets"**: Obviously, and this fits with the markets having an upward bias.

From StockCharts.com:
(www.school.stockcharts.com/doku.php?id=overview:bob_farrell_10_rules), accessed March 13, 2020

Well, you did it! You have reached the end of the book. As you have seen there are a lot of details associated with making money in the stock market by trend trading. Like any other skill, you have to learn this one until all factors feel comfortable and almost second nature. This feeling only comes with practice, and lots of it. Once you have made the plunge with real money you may still make mistakes which is ok since everyone makes mistakes, even those with lots of experience make them. But, you must learn from your mistakes by reviewing what you did wrong so they aren't repeated again.

A few of the concepts may seem to go counter to traditional wisdom like investing 100% of your capital with each trade. Remember, you are only committing a relatively small amount of your money with your first trade which through "Compound Investing" will substantially increase in value over time. This relatively small amount of money should be money you don't need for your everyday life. Only if you feel very comfortable and experienced with this relatively small amount of money would I suggest adding to this investment fund.

Another potentially controversial point is only investing in TQQQ. This point isn't really controversial since you are minimizing your risk by only buying this one ETF which represents the NASDAQ 100 market average and which also represents 100 of the largest tech stocks. Since you are committing to only trade TQQQ you don't have to worry about 3-month earnings surprises to the potential downside or worry if this stock will go down due to factors out of your control. Your money will also increase rapidly since this ETF is triple leveraged which goes up 3X when the NASDAQ 100 goes up 1X.

I would suggest reading this book in its entirety again and making notes in areas you want to pay extra attention to. If you research a stock chart that matches one of the figures in this book, read over the setup and the outcome again.

And, finally, happy investing.

Sincerely,

Made in the USA
Columbia, SC
22 September 2020

21343790R00075